THE UNKNOWN LIFE

OF

JESUS CHRIST

BY THE DISCOVERER OF THE MANUSCRIPT,

NICOLAS NOTOVITCH.

TRANSLATED FROM THE FRENCH BY

ALEXINA LORANGER.

PUBLISHED BY
THE LOST LIBRARY
GLASTONBURY, ENGLAND

First Published by
Rand, McNally & Co. in 1894
This edition 2016

This facsimile edition has been carefully scanned
and reprinted in the traditional manner by
THE LOST LIBRARY
5 High Street,
Glastonbury UK BA6 9DP

The LOST LIBRARY is a publishing house based in
Glastonbury, UK, dedicated to the reproduction
of important rare esoteric and scholarly texts for
the discerning reader.

Cataloguing Information
The Unknown life of Jesus Christ
Nicolas Notovich

ISBN 978 1 90662 139 1

Printed and bound in Great Britain by
Clays Ltd, St Ives plc

THE LOST
LIBRARY

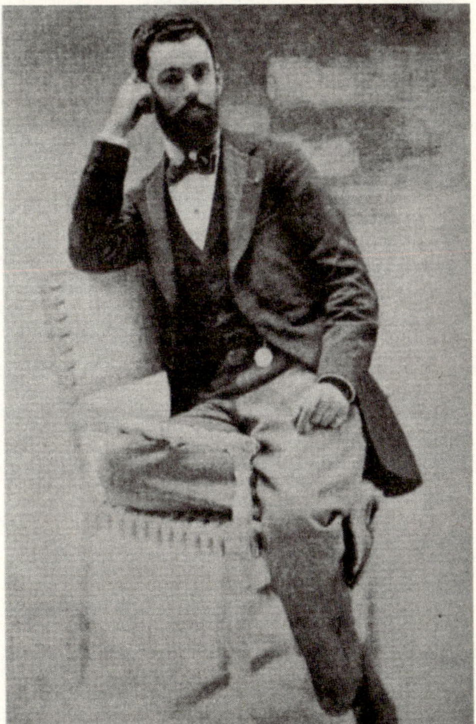

TABLE OF CONTENTS.

PREFACE,	7
A JOURNEY TO THIBET,	13
THE LADAK,	62
A FEAST IN A GONPA,	76
THE LIFE OF SAINT ISSA,	98
EPITOME,	147
EXPLANATORY NOTES,	184

PREFACE.

AFTER the close of the Turko-Russian War (1877-1878) I undertook a series of extended journeys through the Orient. Having visited all points of interest in the Balkan Peninsula, I crossed the Caucasian Mountains into Central Asia and Persia, and finally, in 1887, made an excursion into India, the most admired country of the dreams of my childhood.

The first object of this journey was to study the customs and habits of the inhabitants of India amid their own surroundings, as well as the grand, mysterious archæology and the colossal, majestic nature of the country. Wandering without any settled course from one locality to another, I at last came to mountainous Afghanistan, whence I reached India through the picturesque passes of Bolan and Guernaï. I then followed the Indus to Rawal-Pindi, traveled through the Punjab — the country of five rivers — visited the golden temple of Amritsir, the tomb of Randjid Singh, king of the Punjab, near Lahore, and proceeded toward Kashmir, the "vale of eternal happiness." There I began my peregrinations as fancy or curiosity guided or dictated, until I reached the Ladak, where I intended to make a somewhat lengthy stay before returning to Russia through Eastern Turkestan and Karakorum.

In the course of one of my visits to a Buddhist convent, I learned from the chief Lama that there existed very ancient memoirs, treating of the life of Christ and of the nations of the Occident, in the archives of Lassa, and that a few of the larger monasteries possessed copies and translations of these precious chronicles.

There being little probability of my early return to this country, I resolved to delay my departure for Europe, and verify these assertions by seeing some of these copies, even though I were obliged to invade every convent as far as Lassa — a journey far less perilous and difficult to accomplish than we are usually led to believe. Besides this, I was now so well accustomed to the dangers encountered by the traveler in those regions that they no longer possessed any terrors for me.

During my sojourn in Leh, the capital of Ladak, I visited Himis, a large convent in the outskirts of the city, where I was informed by the Lama that the monastic libraries contained a few copies of the manuscript in question.

PREFACE.

That I might not arouse the suspicions of the authorities in regard to the object of my visit to the convent, and raise no obstacles to a subsequent journey into Thibet — as a Russian — on my return to Leh I announced my immediate departure for India, and again left the capital of Ladak.

An unfortunate accident, whereby my leg was fractured, furnished me with a totally unexpected pretext to enter the monastery, where I received excellent care and nursing; and I took advantage of my short stay among these monks to obtain the privilege of seeing the manuscripts relating to Christ. With the aid of my interpreter, who translated from the Thibetan tongue, I carefully transcribed the verses as they were read by the Lama.

Entertaining no doubt of the authenticity of this narrative, written with the utmost precision by Brahmin historians and Buddhists of India and Nepal, my intention was to publish the translation on my return to Europe. With this object in view, I addressed myself to several well-known ecclesiastics, requesting them to revise my notes and tell me what they thought of the matter.

Monseigneur Platon, the celebrated archbishop of Kiew, believed my discovery to be of great importance; but he earnestly tried to dissuade me from giving the memoirs publicity, declaring it would be against my own interests to do so.

Why? This the venerable prelate refused to explain. Our conversation, however, having taken place in Russia, where censorship would have placed its veto on a work of this kind, I determined to wait.

A year later I chanced to be in Rome. Here I submitted the manuscript to a cardinal standing high in the estimation of the Holy Father.

"Why should you print this?" he said, didactically; "nobody will attach much importance to it, and you will create numberless enemies thereby. You are still young, however. If you need money, I can obtain some compensation for these notes, enough to remunerate you for your loss of time and expenditure." Naturally enough, I refused the offer.

In Paris I laid my project before Cardinal Rotelli, whom I had met in Constantinople. He also opposed the publication of my work, under pretext that it would be premature. "The church," he added, "suffers too deeply from this new current of atheistic ideas; and you would only furnish new food to the calumniators and detractors of the evangelical doctrine. I tell you this in the interest of all Christian churches."

I then called on M. Jules Simon, who found my communication most interesting, and advised me to consult M. Renan in regard to the best means of publishing these memoirs.

The very next day I found myself seated in the study of the great philosopher. At the end of the interview M. Renan proposed that I should intrust him with the memoirs in question, that he might make a report on them to the Academy. This proposition, as the reader will understand, was most seductive and flattering; yet I took away the work with me, saying I wished to revise it once more — the fact being that I feared if I accepted this association I would only receive the bare honor of discovering the chronicles, while the illustrious author of the "Life of Jesus" would reap the glory of the publication and of the commentaries. Believing myself sufficiently prepared to publish the narrative by adding my own notes, I finally declined the courteous offer made to me. That I might not, however, wound the feelings of the great master, whom I deeply respected, I resolved to await his death, which could not be far off, judging from his feebleness. Soon after the death of M. Renan, I wrote to M. Jules Simon, and again sought his advice. His reply was that I should judge for myself of the expediency of giving publicity to the memoirs.

I therefore prepared my notes, and now publish them, reserving the right to attest the authenticity of these chronicles. In my commentaries I carefully develop the arguments which prove the good faith and sincerity of the Buddhist compilers. It only remains for me to add that before criticising my work scientific societies can, without much expense, organize an expedition whose mission it will be to study these manuscripts in the locality in which they are to be found, and thus verify their historical value.

Nicolas Notovitch.

P. S.— In the course of my travels I took many curious photographs, but when I came to examine the negatives on my return to India I was dismayed to find that they were absolutely destroyed.

The Unknown Life of Jesus Christ.

A JOURNEY TO THIBET.

DURING my sojourn in India, I found many opportunities to mingle and converse with the Buddhists; and so thoroughly was my curiosity excited by their accounts of Thibet that I resolved to immediately undertake a journey to that almost unknown country. With this view, I chose a route extending through Kashmir, a country I had often desired to explore.

On October 14, 1887, I took my place in the compartment of a railway train literally filled with soldiers, and traveled from Lahore to Rawal-Pindi, reaching the latter place at noon the following day. Having recovered from the fatigues of the journey and visited the city, which, owing to its permanent garrison, presents the appearance of a war camp, I turned my attention to the purchase of such articles as are necessary on a journey where railways are unknown, and horses furnish the only means of conveyance. With the aid of my negro servant, Pondichery, I packed my luggage, procured a tonga (a two-wheeled vehicle drawn by a pair of horses), and, having made myself as comfortable as circumstances would permit on the rear seat, began my journey over the picturesque route leading to Kashmir.

Our tonga was soon rolling rapidly along the magnificent road, though no little dexterity was required in going through a large caravan of soldiers belonging to a detachment traveling from the camp into the city, with their cumbersome luggage loaded on the backs of camels. Soon we came to the end of the Punjab Valley, and turning into a sinuous path began to climb the Outer Himalayan Range. The acclivity became more and more abrupt as we ascended, while the magnificent panorama stretching away beneath our feet grew less and less distinct. The last rays of the setting sun were gilding the summit of the mountains as our tonga gaily emerged from the winding road on the crest of the mountain, below which nestles the pretty little town of Murree, a summer resort much in favor with the families of English officials, on account of its shade and comparative coolness.

The journey from Murree to Serinagur may be accomplished by tonga; but at the approach of winter, when all Europeans desert Kashmir, the tonga service is suspended. Having undertaken my journey near the end of the warm season, I greatly astonished the English tourists whom I met on their way back to India; but their efforts to discover the object of my journey remained fruitless.

The roadway not being entirely constructed yet, I was obliged, not without considerable difficulty, however, to hire saddle-horses. Night had already fallen when we started on our descent from Murree, which stands at an altitude of five thousand feet. The road was dark, and deeply rutted by recent rains, and the journey was anything but cheerful, as the horses faithfully plodded along, guided by instinct rather than sight. As night deepened, rain began to fall in torrents; and the shadows cast by the century oaks surrounding us shrouded us in impenetrable darkness. Fearing that we might stray apart and get lost, we kept up a continual shouting as we rode on. Above us we knew, though we could not pierce the thick gloom, that gigantic masses of rock overhung the path, while to the left a rushing torrent thundered down over a precipice hidden by the trees.

We had waded through the thick mud for more than two hours, chilled to the bones by the icy rain, when the distant light of a fire at last appeared to revive our strength. But, alas! how very deceiving such lights prove in the wilderness of the mountain! One moment it seems almost within reach of your hand, but suddenly disappears, to reappear, sometimes at your left, then at your right, sometimes above, then below you, as if it took pleasure in tantalizing the weary traveler. Meanwhile, the road makes a thousand turns, zigzagging in every direction, while the motionless fire seems animated with perpetual motion, the obscurity being so dense that we fail to see the continual changes in the direction of the road.

I had regretfully abandoned all hope of ever reaching this so earnestly longed-for fire, when it suddenly reappeared so close to us that the horses involuntarily stopped short.

Here I must pause to express my gratitude and offer my sincere thanks to the English for their kind thoughtfulness in erecting along the roads a number of small bungalows, in which the weary traveler is glad to find shelter and rest. These isolated inns possess little comfort, it is true, but the exhausted pilgrim does not even notice the lack of luxuries, so delighted is he to find a clean dry room in which to stretch his tired limbs.

The Hindoos evidently did not expect travelers at that advanced hour of the night and at that season, for they had carried away the keys, and we were compelled to force open the door of the bungalow.

I immediately threw myself on the bed, which consisted of one pillow and a piece of wet carpet, and was soon buried in slumber. At dawn, after partaking of tea and a little food, we resumed our way under a scorching sun. Now and then we passed through a village, standing in some magnificent defile, or along the winding path that penetrated into the very bosom of the mountains, until we finally reached the Jhelum, whose sparkling waters flow gracefully over a rocky bed, and whose course is confined within a picturesque gorge that sometimes rises almost to the azure vault of the Himalayan heavens— heavens wonderfully pure and serene in this region.

At noon we reached a hamlet called Tongua, where the houses are strung along the river-bank and appear like so many boxes with façade openings. Cosmetics and all kinds of merchandise are retailed. The place literally swarms with Hindoos, each bearing on his brow the diversely colored mark of his particular caste. Here, too, is seen the dignified Kashmirian, clad in a long white tunic and an equally snowy turban.

In consideration of a good round sum of money,

I procured the loan of a Hindoo cabriolet from a Kashmirian. This equipage is so constructed that one must sit with crossed legs, or Turkish fashion, while the seat is so small that it will barely accommodate two persons. The absence of a back, moreover, renders this mode of locomotion extremely dangerous. Such was my anxiety to reach the end of my journey, however, that I unhesitatingly climbed on this circular table — so awkwardly perched on two wheels and drawn by a single horse — rather than delay my departure one unnecessary day.

But I had barely gone a half-kilometer when I seriously began to regret my saddle-horse, so fatiguing and difficult did I find it to keep my legs crossed and maintain my equilibrium. Unfortunately, it was too late to turn back.

Night had fallen when I arrived at Horis, exhausted with fatigue and bruised by the jolting, my limbs feeling as though they were the central point of attack from millions of ants, and too utterly wretched to enjoy the picturesque scenery opening before our eyes as we advanced along the Jhelum, on the banks of which arises a chain of wooded mountains on one side, while the other is bordered by a rocky precipice.

At Horis I met a caravan of pilgrims on their way from Mecca. Imagining that I was a physician, and hearing of my hurry to reach the Ladak, they begged me to join them, which I promised to do after reaching Serinagur.

I left the village on horseback at dawn, after a night spent seated upright on my bed, holding a lighted torch in my hand, and not daring to close my eyes, lest I should be stung by the myriads of scorpions and centipedes which infested the bungalows. Though heartily ashamed of the terror inspired in me by those insects, I could not sufficiently overcome it to compose myself to sleep.

Who can point out the dividing-line between courage and cowardice? Who can say where the one begins and the other ends?

I make no boast of bravery, but I am not a coward. And yet, the insurmountable fear aroused in me by that species of small animals totally banished sleep from my eyes in spite of my extreme fatigue.

As our horses slowly advanced through the flat valley, with the sun beaming warmly on us from over the mountains, I gradually fell asleep in the saddle. I was suddenly aroused by a chilly breeze some time later, and found that we were ascending a mountain-path in the midst of a vast forest, which sometimes opened to give us a glimpse of an impetuous torrent, with picturesque surroundings, then quickly closed again, concealing from our view the mountains, the sky, the entire country in fact, but giving us instead the songs of myriads of its bright-plumaged birds.

We emerged from the forest at about noon, descended into a small hamlet on the river-bank, and having refreshed ourselves with a cold lunch, resumed the journey. As we passed the market-place I stopped with the intention of purchasing a glass of warm milk from a Hindoo who was squatting beside a large pail of boiling milk; but what was my surprise when he proposed that I should take the pail with its contents, declaring that I had defiled the liquid.

"I only want a glass of milk, not the pail," I explained.

"According to our laws," replied the Hindoo, "if any one not belonging to our caste gazes fixedly at any object, or article of food, we must throw away the one and wash the other. You have defiled my milk, O Sahib, and no one will drink it; for not only did you gaze at it, but you also pointed your finger in its direction."

Having long examined his merchandise to make sure it was real milk, as well as pointed out from which side of the pail I desired to have it poured, I stood convicted; and as I always respect the laws and customs of strange nations, I readily gave him a rupee, the full price of the spilt milk, although I had taken but one glass. The incident taught me a lesson, however, and I was never again guilty of fixing my eyes on the food of a Hindoo.

There is no religious doctrine more encumbered with ceremonies, laws, and commentaries than Brahminism. While each religion possesses but one Bible, one gospel, or one Koran, from which the Hebrews, the Christians, and the Mohammedans borrow their faith, the Brahmin Hindoos possess so great a number of commentaries in folio that the most learned Brahmin that ever existed scarcely had time to reach the tenth.

Leaving aside the four books of the Vedas, the Pouranas, written in Sanscrit, and composed of eighteen volumes, containing four hundred thousand stanzas, which treat of law, theology, medicine, of the creation, the destruction and regeneration of the world, etc.; the vast Chastras, which treat of mathematics, grammar, etc.; the Oupovedas, Oupanichadas, Oupopouranas, which serve as explanation to the Pouranas, and a host of other commentaries in many volumes, there still remain the twelve large books containing the laws of Manou, grandson of Brahma. These books not only relate to penal and civil laws, but also to canonical regulations, which impose on their adepts such an infinite number of ceremonies that we can not but admire the unalterable patience of the Hindoos in their observation of the precepts dictated by Saint Manou.

Manou was incontestably a great legislator and profound thinker, but he has written so extensively that he frequently contradicts himself in the same page. The Brahmins do not even remark this, and the poor Hindoos, whose mission it is to labor for the support of that caste, humbly obey their clergy, whose commands enjoin them to never touch a man not belonging to their own caste; while a stranger is absolutely forbidden to fix his attention on anything owned by the Hindoos.

By this adherence to the strict sense of the law, the Hindoo imagines that his food is contaminated when it becomes the point of attraction to a stranger. And yet, even as late as the period of its second birth, Brahminism was a purely monotheistic religion, recognizing but one infinite and indivisible God. But, as in all ages and religions, the clergy, taking advantage of their privileged position, gradually enacted laws of their own and instituted different forms of external worship, hoping thereby to influence the ignorant masses.

By degrees, the principles of monotheism — of which so clear a conception is given by the Vedas — degenerated into an absurd, unlimited series of gods, goddesses, semi-gods, genii, angels, and demons, all represented by idols as varied in form as they are repulsive to the sight. These people, formerly as proud as their religion was pure and grand, are now drifting into a complete state of idiocy, the day scarcely sufficing for the accomplishment of all the duties prescribed by the ecclesiastical laws.

It may well be positively asserted that the Hindoos subsist merely to provide for the principal sect of Brahmins, who have grasped the temporal power formerly held by the independent sovereigns of the people. While governing India, the English never interfere with this phase of public life, and the Brahmins take advantage of this to inspire in the nation the hope of a better future.

The sun soon vanished behind the towering peaks, and the shadows of night immediately fell over the picturesque scenery we were traversing. The deep hush of sleep then also spread over the narrow valley lapped by the Jhelum. The road, winding along a narrow ledge of steep rocks, insensibly melted from our view, mountains and trees became one confused somber mass, and the stars began to peep from the sky above. We alighted from our horses and groped our way along the mountain-sides, fearing every moment to be dashed into the yawning precipice at our feet.

At an advanced hour of the night we crossed a bridge and climbed up a steep incline leading to the Ouri bungalow, which stands in complete isolation on those heights. The following day we traversed a charming region; still skirting the river-bank, we came to a sharp bend, where we found the ruins of a Saic fortress, seemingly grieving over the ashes of its glorious past. In a small valley, almost concealed in the midst of the surrounding mountains, we found a bungalow, with its door invitingly opened in welcome; and not far away we suddenly came into the camp of a cavalry regiment belonging to the army of the Maharaja of Kashmir.

On learning that I was a Russian, the officers courteously invited me to breakfast with them. It was on this occasion that I had the pleasure of forming the acquaintance of Colonel Brown, who was the first to compile a dictionary of the Afghan-Pouchtou tongue.

Being extremely anxious to reach Serinagur as soon as possible, I at once resumed my journey, through a most picturesque region lying at the foot of the mountains. To my eyes, so wearied by the monotony of the preceding scenery, the inhabited valley that now stretched before us, with its two-story buildings, its gardens, and cultivated fields, came as a positive relief. At a short distance, hidden by a range of high hillocks, which we crossed toward evening, begins the celebrated "Vale of Kashmir."

How can I describe the magnificent scenery that opened before my eyes as I reached the brow of the last hill that separates the "Vale of Kashmir" from the mountainous country I had just traversed! A dazzling picture held me spellbound!

The "Vale of Kashmir," which is everywhere populated, and whose limits are lost in the horizon, is walled in by the high Himalaya Mountains. At the rising and setting of the sun the zone of eternal snows appears like a silver ring encircling this rich, beautiful plateau, which is intersected by many fine roads and numberless sparkling rivers.

The gardens, the hillocks, and the lake, with its many islands covered with buildings of presumptuous style, all contribute to make the traveler believe he has been suddenly transported into another world. He is strongly inclined to tarry here forever, thinking he must have found the paradise, or enchanted land, of his nursery days.

The veil of night soon spread over the valley, merging mountains, gardens, and lakes into one dark mass, with a few distant lights glimmering here and there like stars. I descended the valley in the direction of the Jhelum, which has cut its way through a narrow defile in the mountains to unite its waters with those of the River Indus.

A legend exists in which it is claimed that the valley was once an inland sea, the waters of which forced a passage through the environing prison-walls, leaving no trace but a few small ponds and the Jhelum River, which empties into the Indus. Its banks are almost hidden by the numerous long, narrow boats which serve as shelter for the families of the owners the year round.

From this point, Serinagur may be reached in one day on horseback, but the journey by boat consumes a day and a half. I nevertheless chose to travel by water; and having procured a boat, after much haggling about prices with the proprietor, I installed myself at its prow on a piece of carpet, protected by a sort of awning.

We left at midnight, the boat gliding toward Serinagur. At the other extremity of the bark a Hindoo was quietly preparing me a cup of tea, while I fell into a dreamless sleep, happy in the thought that I was advancing on my journey without further exertion and fatigue.

I was aroused by the warm caresses of the rising sun, and opened my eyes on a glimpse of nature that charmed me into ecstasies: a bank of velvety verdure; the distant outlines of snow-capped peaks; pretty villages, nestling at the foot of the mountain; a crystalline sheet of water; a pure, balmy atmosphere, which I breathed with avidity; the warbling of an infinity of birds; a sky of transcendent purity; behind me the swish of the water under the impulsion of a rounded oar dexterously handled by a beautiful woman, with wonderful eyes and cheeks delicately bronzed by the sun. All these cast a spell upon me, and I totally forgot the reason of my presence there. In that one moment I ceased to long for the end of my journey; and yet, what endless privations and perils there still remained to face and endure! The boat glided swiftly down the stream, the magnificent scenery unceasingly unfolding before my eyes to melt away beyond the confines of the horizon, where it seemingly became part of the mountains already passed; then, far away, in the direction toward which we were drifting, another glorious picture seemed to unroll from the mountain-side, a picture that grew more and more vivid as we were carried onward.

Twilight was now gathering fast about us, and still I did not weary of the contemplation of this glorious bit of nature, which awakened in my heart the sweetest recollections of my youth and childhood. How beautiful indeed were those days, now forever gone!

As we neared Serinagur we saw more and more of those pretty villages buried in verdure.

As the boat came to a stop a number of people flocked to the river-bank, the men wearing turbans, the women in small caps, and long chemises reaching to the ground, and the children in a state of nudity that strongly reminded us of the garments in vogue with our first parents.

A long row of boats and floating houses, in which dwell entire families, lines the stream at the entrance of the city. As we quietly glided between these wooden huts the last rays of the setting sun were gilding the snow-covered summits of the distant mountains.

Life here seems to cease with the setting of the sun. Thousands of gaily colored dungas and banglas (boats), adorned with palanquins, were moored to the quay, while Kashmirians of both sexes, attired in the primitive costume of Adam and Eve, were performing their twilight ablutions absolutely unrestrained by the presence of others; for the importance of the rite they were executing was far greater to them than that of all human prejudices.

On the morning of October 20th I opened my eyes in a clean cozy room overlooking the river, which sparkled and glistened beneath the glorious sun of Kashmir. My object not being to describe my voyage in these pages, I will say nothing of the valleys, the paradise of lilacs; of the enchanted islands, the many historical palaces, the picturesque pagodas, so redolent of mystery; the coquettish villages, seemingly lost in vast gardens; or of the majestic peaks of the giants of the Himalaya, rising on all sides and buried beneath a white shroud of eternal snow. I shall merely note the preparations made in view of a new journey in the direction of Thibet. I spent six days in Serinagur, making long excursions into its beautiful surrounding country, examining the numerous ruins that still stand as evidence of the ancient prosperity of that region, and studying the curious customs of the land.

The Kashmir, as well as the other provinces attached to it, such as the Baltistan, the Ladak, etc., are vassals of England. They formerly made part of the possessions of the "Lion of Punjab," Randjid Sing; but at his death English troops invaded Lahore, the capital of the

Punjab, separated Kashmir from the rest of the empire, and under pretense of hereditary possession and in consideration of one hundred and sixty millions of francs, ceded it to Goubab-Sing, a relation of the dead sovereign, on whom was conferred the title of Maharaja. At the time of my voyage, the reigning Maharaja was Pertab-Sing, grandson of Goubab, who resides in Jamooee, on the southern slope of the Himalayas.

The celebrated "Vale of Kashmir," which is eighty-five miles in length and twenty-five miles in breadth, enjoyed its days of true glory and prosperity during the reign of the Great Mogul, whose court gathered there to enjoy the rustic pleasures of the country in the cottages still standing on the small islands of the lake.

A large number of the Maharajas of Hindoostan formerly spent the summer months here also, and took part in the sumptuous round of festivities given by the Great Mogul; but time has wrought a woful change, and the "happy valley" is now nothing more than a place of resort for mendicants. Weeds and the moldiness from all sorts of noxious plants have covered the limpid water of the lake, the wild juniper bush has choked all vegetation on the islands, palaces and pavilions have nothing left but the remembrance of their dead grandeur, dust and rank growths overspread the ruins like a mantle. The surrounding mountains, with their white pinnacles, seem mournfully sad and patiently waiting for better days to burst forth in all their immortal beauty. The inhabitants, hitherto intellectual, handsome, and cleanly, are tending toward a state of idiocy; being filthy and lazy, and governed by the lash instead of the sword. The Kashmirians have so frequently been exposed to pillage and invasion, and have known so many masters, that they have become indifferent to everything; spending their time near their huts or on the river bank gossiping, or quietly making their celebrated shawls and cutting designs on gold or silver. The women are extremely melancholy, and bear an expression of inconceivable sadness on their features. Misery and squalor reign everywhere. The fine men and beautiful women of Kashmir are filthy and ragged beyond conception; and the dress of both sexes, in winter and summer alike, consists only of a long heavy gown, with wide flowing sleeves, resembling nothing more than a shirt. This garment is removed only when completely worn out, and never — under any consideration — is it washed, giving the white turbans of the male population a dazzling whiteness in contrast with their stained, greasy gowns.

A deep sadness overcomes the traveler as he notes the contrast between this rich, opulent country and its ragged inhabitants.

Serinagur (the city of the sun), or Cashmere as it is sometimes called from the name of the country, is the capital and is situated on the Jhelum, along the bank of which it extends southward over a distance of five kilometers.

The two-story houses, which shelter a population of one hundred thousand inhabitants, are constructed of wood, and stand in close proximity to the water. The town itself is not more than two kilometers in breadth, and everybody lives on the river whose banks are united by ten or twelve bridges. Steps lead from every house to the waters of the Jhelum, where nearly the entire day is spent in ablutions, bathing, and washing utensils — the latter consisting merely of two or three brass jugs. A portion of the inhabitants practice the Mohammedan religion, while two-thirds are Brahmans; there are also a few Buddhists, though the number is extremely limited.

The time had now arrived to begin my preparations for a journey into the unknown. Having purchased different kinds of conserves, a few casks of wine, and many other things found indispensable in the course of a journey through a country as sparsely populated as Thibet, I

A JOURNEY TO THIBET.

packed the whole in boxes, hired ten carriers and one interpreter, bought myself a horse, and fixed the date of departure for October 27th. To enliven the road I procured from a Frenchman, Monsiur Peicheau, superintendent of the Maharaja's vineyard, a large dog which had already accompanied my friends Bonvalot, Capus, and Pepin, the well-known explorers through the Pamir. Wishing to shorten the journey by two days, I started the carriers at dawn from the other side of the lake, while I crossed by boat, rejoining the caravan and my horse at the foot of the chain of mountains that separated the Serinagur Valley from the Gorge of the Sindh.

Never shall I forget the tortures we endured in climbing, almost on all fours, to the summit of a peak three thousand feet high. The carriers were exhausted and out of breath, and I trembled lest one of them might roll down the declivity at any moment with his burden, while my heart fairly ached at sight of my poor dog, Pamir, who stumbled along with his tongue lolling out, whining and falling by the way at every few steps. I forgot my own fatigue to caress and encourage the poor animal, who looked at me piteously, bravely went on a few steps more, and again fell exhausted.

Night had fallen when we reached the pinnacle

of the mountain, where we greedily flung ourselves on the snow to quench our thirst. Having taken a brief rest, we began the descent through a dense pine forest, hoping to gain the village of Haïena at the foot of the defile before the appearance of beasts of prey.

A straight well-kept road leads from Serinagur to Haïena, going directly north to Ganderbal, where it turns abruptly to the east, after having skirted the Sindh and traversed a country of luxurious vegetation to Kangan, which is six miles from Haïena; toward which place I was journeying by a more direct route through a pass three thousand feet high, but which saved both time and distance.

My first steps into the unknown were marked by an incident that left a most horrible impression upon me. The defile of the Sindh, which is sixty miles long, is particularly celebrated for its inhospitable inhabitants, among which panthers, tigers, leopards, black bears, wolves, and jackals abound. The snow having unfortunately just spread its white mantle over the summits of the chain, these redoubtable foes of man had been forced to seek shelter in their lairs somewhat lower down.

We were silently following the narrow winding path through the pines and centenary birch trees, the grinding sound of our footsteps alone breaking the deep monotonous hush of the night, when suddenly, in our very midst as it seemed, a prolonged howl awoke the echoes of the forest. Our little band stopped short and listened.

"A panther!" gasped my servant, who stood trembling by my side.

The small caravan of twelve men stood with bated breath, paralyzed with fear. I now remembered that at our last resting place I had entrusted my revolver to one of the carriers and given my rifle to another; the thought filled me with poignant regret and alarm, and I inquired in a low tone for one of these men. A more terrible cry rang through the night at this moment, then a crash like the fall of a heavy body was heard, succeeded by a shriek of agony that froze the blood in our veins. We guessed rather than saw the horrible struggle going on between the unfortunate man and the famished beast of prey.

"Sahib, take the gun," whispered a voice near me.

I feverishly clutched the Winchester. But, alas, I could not see two feet from me. Another cry, followed by a stifled roar, guided me; and I crept in its direction, equally divided between my desire to kill a panther and the horrible dread of being flayed alive. Nobody dared to move; and it was not until fully five minutes had elapsed that one of the men thought of lighting a match.

Remembering the dread of fire usually evinced by wild beasts, I then caught up a few handfuls of brush-wood and set flame to it.

Not more than ten feet from us, we then saw the unfortunate victim stretched on the ground, his limbs completely torn away by the claws of a beautiful panther which still crouched unmoved with a piece of flesh between its jaws. Near by lay a cask of wine completely crushed.

Scarcely had I shouldered my gun, however, when the beast of prey sprang to its feet, dropped its bleeding morsel of food and turned as if ready to leap upon me; then with a blood-curdling howl, it suddenly veered about and disappeared in the thicket.

My coolies, who all this time had been prostrated to the ground by terror, now gradually recovered from their fright and prepared to go on. Having gathered a bunch of dry underbrush, placed some matches at hand, and cocked our guns, we hurried toward Haïena, leaving the remains of the unfortunate Hindoo behind us in fear of sharing the same fate.

One hour later, we came out of the forest into the open country. I immediately had my tent put up under a leafy plane-tree and an enormous fire built; this being the only means of protection that could be used against the wild beasts whose howls came from every direction about us freezing the blood in our veins. Meanwhile my dog crouched trembling at my feet; but, once in the tent, he quickly regained his courage and spent the rest of the night in incessant barking.

That night was a terrible one to me, as I sat upright with my rifle clutched tightly in my hand, listening to the horrible howling and roaring that filled the air with deafening echoes. A few panthers approached our camp in response to Pamir's bark, but none dared to come within shooting distance.

I had left Serinagur at the head of eleven carriers, of whom four carried as many casks of wine, four more the clothes needed for the journey, another my weapons, and still another different utensils, while a last served as courier and guide, as he frequently went forward to reconnoiter. The latter's name was Chicari, which signifies, "he who accompanies the hunter and picks up the game." But owing to his cowardice and utter ignorance of the country, I dismissed him, with some of the other men the next morning, retaining only four carriers with me. I quickly replaced them with horses, and slowly proceeded toward the village of Gounde.

What beautiful nature unfolds itself in the gorge of the Sindh, and how beloved it is by the hunter. Besides the larger beasts of prey, there are also found deer, moufflon, and an immense variety of birds, among which may be mentioned the golden, the red, and the snow-white pheasant, large partridges, and immense eagles.

The villages along the Sindh are not remarkable for their dimensions, most of them consisting of but ten to twenty wretched huts, occupied by ragged families that bear the stamp of poverty. The domestic animals all belong to an exceedingly small species.

Crossing the stream at Sambal I stopped near the Gounde village for a relay of horses. In some of the small places, I was absolutely refused a change of horses until I made use of my whip, a proceeding which at once imposed respect and obedience. Money also proved a most powerful agent in attaining this object, inspiring a servile obedience and a desire to execute my orders that was truly astonishing.

Gold and the lash are the real sovereigns of the Orient; without them the Great Mogul himself could have had no preponderance.

Meanwhile, night was gathering fast and I was anxious to cross the defile that separates the villages of Gogangan and Sonamarg, the road being in a horrible condition and infested with wild beasts that come to the very doors of the dwelling houses in search of prey under cover of night. The spot is fertile and beautiful, yet few dare make it their home on account of the frequent visits of the panther among the domestic animals.

At the extremity of the defile, near Tchokodar, or Thajwas, I caught sight of two dark masses which I could not at first distinguish in the semi-obscurity, but which, on closer inspection, proved to be two bears following a cub on the roadway. Being alone with my servant — the caravan having remained behind — I hesitated somewhat in attacking them with my single rifle, but long excursions on the mountains had strongly developed the instincts of the hunter in me, and I resolved to brave the dangers. To leap from the saddle, fire, and reload, without even verifying the result of the first shot, was the work of a second. One of the bears sprang toward me, but a second shot changed his course, and he disappeared. Still holding my loaded rifle, I cautiously advanced in the direction in which I had fired and found a bear lying on its side, with a young cub playing near. Another shot brought him down in his turn, and I thus procured two beautiful skins of jet black.

This meeting delayed us two full hours, and night had completely fallen when I pitched my tent near Tchokodar, which I again left at the first streak of dawn for Baltal, still following the course of the Sindh.

The magnificent scenery of the "golden prairie" comes to an abrupt end here with a village of the same name—sona (gold) and marg (prairie). The slope of Zodgi-la is then immediately reached—a steep elevation of eleven thousand five hundred feet—beyond which the entire country assumes a severe, inhospitable character. My hunting adventures were now at an end, having seen nothing this side of Baltal but wild goats. Game might have been found in plenty by penetrating into the very heart of these mysterious mountains, but I had neither the time nor desire to leave the highway on such dangerous expeditions, and I tranquilly continued my journey toward Ladak.

What an abrupt transition I experienced, in passing from the smiling nature and fine population of Kashmir to the barren gloomy rocks and deformed beardless inhabitants of the Ladak!

The country into which I had just penetrated stands at an altitude of eleven to twelve thousand feet, descending to a level of eight thousand at **Kargil.**

The ascent of Zodgi-La is extremely difficult, being an almost perpendicular wall, while, at some points, the road winds over projecting rocks not more than a meter in breadth, bordering on a precipice of unfathomable depth. Heaven preserve the traveler from a fall! In some places long poles have been introduced into the rocks and covered with earth. Brr—! At the thought that the dislodging of the smallest stone from the mountain-side, or the oscillation of the poles might precipitate the structure into the yawning abyss below, carrying with it the intrepid person who might have ventured on this perilous path, my heart almost stopped its beating, and it was with a sigh of relief that I finally came to the end of the dangerous path.

Having crossed the glaciers, we made a halt in the valley and began preparations to spend the night near a post-hut, amid cheerless surroundings of eternal ice and snow.

Beyond Baltal distance is determined by means of daks — postal stations established to facilitate the forwarding of mail. These are low huts situated at a distance of seven kilometers from each other, where a man remains permanently on duty in each. The postal service between the Kashmir and Thibet is of the most primitive kind. The letters are inclosed in a leather bag and placed in charge of a carrier, who rapidly travels over the seven kilometers allotted to him with a basket strapped to his back containing a number of these bags. This he hands over to another carrier, who, in his turn, accomplishes his task in a similar fashion. Neither rain nor snow can stop them, and the service is thus carried on with regularity between Kashmir and Thibet, and vice-versa, once a week. Each run is paid for at the rate of six annas (one franc), this being the compensation usually given merchandise carriers, although my servants carried a burden ten times as heavy. One is filled with compassion at sight of the pale, haggard faces of these weary men; but what can be done? It is the custom of the country, and strangers are powerless. Tea is brought from China in a similar way, a rapid and cheap means of transportation.

As we approached Montaiyan, I rejoined the caravan of Yarkandians which I had promised to accompany on their journey. They recognized me from afar and begged me to examine one of their companions who was very ill. I found him struggling in the throes of a burning fever, and waved my hands as a sign of despair; pointing to heaven to make them understand that human science and will was powerless now, and that God alone could save him. As they were journeying very slowly, I left them once more with the intention of reaching Dras that evening, a town built in the depth of the valley on a river of the same name, near which is a small fort of extremely ancient construction, newly plastered, and guarded by three soldiers of the Maharaja's army.

Here I took shelter in the postal building; the only station in connection with the telegraphic wire laid from Serinagur to the heart of the Himalayas. From this time forward, I totally abandoned my tent at night and sought repose in the roadside inns, which, though repulsively filthy, could always boast of a huge chimney fire.

From Dras to Kargil the scenery is monotonous and disagreeable. The sunrise and sunset are glorious it is true, and the moonlight is magnificent, but the road is flat, endless, and beset with dangers.

Kargil is the chief town of the district and the residence of the governor of the division. The site is decidedly picturesque. Two turbulent streams, the Sourou and Wakka, dash noisely over their rocky beds and unite their rippling waters as they emerge from their respective gorges thus forming the Suru River, on the banks of which the mud buildings of Kargil are constructed. A small fort, guarded by two or three soldiers, stands at the junction of the two streams.

Having procured fresh horses, I resumed my journey at sunrise by entering the Ladak, or Little Thibet. During this day's journey I crossed a shaky bridge, which, like all bridges in Kashmir, was rudely constructed of long beams resting on either banks, overlaid with fagots and slender poles, giving it the appearance of a somewhat primitive suspension bridge. Before long I reached a small plateau over which the road stretched for two kilometers, then gradually descended into the narrow valley of the Wakka, with its many tiny villages, the most picturesque of which is Paskium on the left bank of the river.

I was now treading Buddhist soil. The inhabitants of this part of the country are of the most simple and gentle character, seeming utterly in ignorance of what we term "quarreling" at home. Women are somewhat scarce; but the few we chanced to meet, by the expression of cheerfulness and prosperity reflected upon their countenances, presented a strong contrast to those I had so far seen in Kashmir or India. But this is not astonishing, since each of these women legitimately possesses from three to five husbands.

Polyandry is practiced throughout the country. However large a family may be, there is but one woman in the household; and if it does not consist of more than three persons, a bachelor may become a member of it by bringing material compensation into the house. The days allotted to each of the husbands are determined upon beforehand, and all perform their duties with scrupulous exactitude. The men, as a rule, are of weakly constitutions, with stooped shoulders and a general debilitated appearance, and scarcely ever pass middle age. In fact, I did not meet one single white-haired old man throughout my journey in the Ladak country.

That portion of the Kargil route which lies in the center of the Ladak, is of a more cheerful aspect than the country over which I had just traveled, being much enlivened by a number of small hamlets, but trees and verdure are unfortunately exceedingly scarce.

Twenty miles from Kargil, at the mouth of the defile formed by the swift current of the Wakka, is a small village called Chargol, in the center of which are three altars decked in bright colors (t'hortènes is the name they bear in Thibet). Below, near the river, is a mass of rocks forming long, thick walls, on which flat stones of divers colors have been thrown pell-mell, in the greatest disorder. These stones are elaborately engraved with all sorts of prayers in Sanscrit, Thibetan, and Oudhist characters; and even Arabic inscriptions have sometimes been found in this mixture. Unperceived by my carriers, I surreptitiously abstracted a few of these stones which I subsequently placed in the palace of the Trocadero.

From Chargol on, these peculiar oblong piers are seen at every step. At the first streak of dawn I started on my way with fresh horses, coming to a halt near the convent (gonpa) of Moulbeck, which stands against a tall isolated rock overlooking the hamlet of Wakkha. Not far away towers another gigantic rock of peculiar form, which looks as if transported there by human hands, and bears on one side a carved image of Buddha several meters in height.

On this rock were placed a number of weathercocks that served as a means of invocation. These labor-saving devices consist of wooden hoops draped with white or yellow material, and attached to a stick set vertically into the ground. The softest breeze will set them in motion, and the happy individual who possesses one of these contrivances is no longer obliged to recite his prayers, as everything that may be asked of the presiding god, by the believer, is written thereon.

Seen from a distance this white-plastered monastery, standing in such strong relief against the gray rocks, and these whirling machines with their floating draperies, produce a very strange effect in that half-dead country.

Leaving my horses in the hamlet, and followed by my servant, I turned my steps in the direction of the convent, which was reached by a narrow stairway hewn into the solid rock. At the top of this steep flight, I was greeted by a corpulent Lama, with a fringe of scraggy beard beneath his chin — a characteristic of the Thibetan people — and exceedingly ugly features, but who received me with the utmost cordiality. His dress consisted of a yellow robe and a cloth cap of the same color with ear-laps. In his right hand he carried a brass prayer-wheel, which he set in motion from time to time without the least pause in the conversation. This constituted a perpetual prayer, which being communicated to the air was the more easily wafted to heaven by the aid of the elements. After crossing a long succession of low rooms, in which were shelved a variety of images of Buddha, all sorts and sizes buried beneath a thick mantle of dust, we finally emerged upon an open terrace, from which the eye rested on a most barren waste, interspersed with ledges of gray rocks, and traversed by a single road lost in both directions beyond the limits of the horizon.

We were scarcely seated when an attendant appeared with hop-beer, or tchang, as it is called in this region, prepared within the walls of the monastery. This beverage gives the monks a quantity of superfluous flesh, which is considered by the people as a sign of particular favor from heaven.

The Thibetan language is generally spoken here. The origin of this tongue is enveloped in obscurity; the accepted theory, however, is that a king of Thibet, who reigned in the days of Mohammed, undertook the creation of a universal language to be used by all the followers of Buddha. With this end in view he simplified the Sanscrit grammar, composed an alphabet containing an infinite number of signs, and thus formed the basis of a tongue of exceedingly easy pronunciation, but of most complicated orthography; no less than eight characters being required to represent a single sound. The modern literature of Thibet is all written in this language. The Thibetan tongue in its purity, moreover, is spoken in the Ladak and in Oriental Thibet only; a dialect formed from a mixture of the mother tongue and a variety of idioms borrowed from the people of adjacent regions being used in all other parts of the country.

A JOURNEY TO THIBET.

There always exist two tongues, even in everyday life, among the Thibetans; one being utterly incomprehensible to the women, while the other is spoken by the entire nation. The Thibetan tongue, in all its purity and integrity, can be found in the monasteries only.

The monks much prefer European visitors to Mohammedans; and when I asked the reason of this preference, the Lama replied:

"The Mohammedans have nothing in common with our religion. In their recent victorious campaign, they converted, by force, a number of Buddhists to Islamism; and it will require great efforts on our part to bring back these descendants of Buddhists into the path of the true God. As to Europeans, it is an entirely different matter. Not only do they profess the essential principles of monotheism, but they also form part of the rank of worshipers of Buddha in almost the same degree as the Thibetan Lamas themselves. The only error of the Christians is that after adopting the great doctrine of Buddha, they, at the very outset, completely separated themselves from him and created another Dalaï-Lama; while ours alone has received the divine favor of seeing the majesty of Buddha face to face, and the power of serving as intermediary between heaven and earth."

"Who is this Dalaï-Lama of the Christians of whom you speak?" I asked. "We have a 'Son of God' to whom we address our fervent prayers. It is to him we have recourse, that he may intercede for us near our one and indivisible God."

"It is not to him I referred, sahib," he replied. "We also respect him whom you recognize as the son of an only God, only we do not regard him as such, but as the excellent being, the chosen one from among all. Buddha did, indeed, incarnate himself with his intelligence in the sacred person of Issa, who, without the aid of fire and sword, went forth to propagate our great and true religion through the entire world. I speak of your terrestrial Dalaï-Lama, to whom you have given the title of Father of the Church. There lies the great sin; may it be remitted to the sheep that have strayed from the fold into the evil path," concluded the Lama fervently, as he once more set his prayer-wheel in motion.

I understood that he alluded to the Pope.

"You have said that a son of Buddha, Issa, the chosen one, propagated your religion throughout the world. Who then is he?" I inquired.

The Lama opened his eyes in profound amazement at this question, and muttered something I could not catch, then murmured almost unintelligibly:

"Issa is a great prophet, one of the first after the twenty-two Buddhas; he is greater than any of the Dalaï-Lamas, for he constitutes a part of the spirituality of the Lord. It is he who has instructed you, who has brought back frivolous souls to God, who has rendered you worthy of the blessings of the Creator, who has endowed each creature with the knowledge of good and evil. His name and his deeds have been recorded in our sacred writings, and, whilst reading of his great existence spent in the midst of erring people, we weep over the horrible sin of the pagans, who assassinated him after putting him to the most cruel tortures."

I was forcibly struck by the Lama's words — the prophet Issa, his tortures and death, our Christian Dalaï-Lama, the recognition of Christianity by the Buddhists, all combined to make me think more and more of the career of Jesus Christ — and I begged my interpreter to omit nothing of the Lama's conversation.

"Where are these sacred writings, and by whom were they compiled?" I asked.

"The principal rolls," said the monk, "written in India and Nepal at different epochs, according to the course of events, are at Lassa and number many thousands. In some of the larger convents, there are copies made by the

Lamas at different periods during their stay at Lassa, and later presented to their convents as souvenirs of their visits to the great master, our Dalaï-Lama."

"Do you not possess any of these copies relating to the prophet Issa?"

"No, we do not possess any. Our convent is of little importance, and the Lamas have collected but a few hundred manuscripts since its foundation. The large cloisters possess thousands of them, but they are sacred things, and you can not see them anywhere."

After a few minutes more conversation, I returned to the camp, reflecting deeply on what had been said by the Lama.

Issa, the prophet of Buddhists! How could that have been? Being of Jewish origin, he dwelt in Palestine and Egypt; and the scripture contains not a word, not the slightest allusion to the part played by Buddhism in the education of Jesus.

I determined to visit every convent in Thibet, hoping to gather more ample information concerning the prophet Issa and perhaps find copies of documents relating to him.

Without being aware of it, we traversed the Namykala Pass at an altitude of thirteen thousand feet, from which we descended into the val-

Lamas at different periods during their stay at Lassa, and later presented to their convents as souvenirs of their visits to the great master, our Dalaï-Lama."

"Do you not possess any of these copies relating to the prophet Issa?"

"No, we do not possess any. Our convent is of little importance, and the Lamas have collected but a few hundred manuscripts since its foundation. The large cloisters possess thousands of them, but they are sacred things, and you can not see them anywhere."

After a few minutes more conversation, I returned to the camp, reflecting deeply on what had been said by the Lama.

Issa, the prophet of Buddhists! How could that have been? Being of Jewish origin, he dwelt in Palestine and Egypt; and the scripture contains not a word, not the slightest allusion to the part played by Buddhism in the education of Jesus.

I determined to visit every convent in Thibet, hoping to gather more ample information concerning the prophet Issa and perhaps find copies of documents relating to him.

Without being aware of it, we traversed the Namykala Pass at an altitude of thirteen thousand feet, from which we descended into the val-

the dry bed of a torrent, I descended into a hamlet called Lamayure, which springs up unexpectedly before the eyes of the traveler. A convent, seemingly glued to the face of the rocky cliff and held there by miraculous intervention, dominates the village. Stairways are unknown in this monastery, ropes being used to ascend and descend from one floor to another; and the only means of communication with the outer world is through an endless labyrinth of passages and corridors. Directly beneath the convent windows, which appear like huge nests suspended from an isolated rock, is a small inn of uninviting aspect which offers little comfort to the traveler. Hardly had I stretched myself upon the carpet in my room when it was invaded by a number of yellow-robed monks, who questioned me closely regarding the object of my journey, the country from which I came, etc., concluding by inviting me to accompany them.

In spite of my fatigue, I accepted the invitation and followed them up the steep passages hewn in the solid rock, encumbered by an infinity of prayer-wheels which I involuntarily set in motion as I passed. These devices are thus placed to save the passer-by any loss of time in prayer; and a stranger might be led to suppose that **worldly** affairs absorbed their entire day, leaving

A JOURNEY TO THIBET. 55

no time for prayer. Many pious Buddhists utilize the current of rivers for this purpose; and I have frequently seen long rows of these cylinders, covered with invocations, placed on river banks, so that the steady flow of water might keep them in constant movement, and thus exempt their owners from the obligation of praying.

I finally found myself seated on a bench in a dimly lighted room, whose walls were adorned with the inevitable statues of Buddha, books, and prayer-wheels, with the loquacious monks eagerly explaining the signification of each object.

"And these volumes treat of religion, no doubt?" I ventured, during a pause.

"Yes," was the reply; "they treat of the first and principal rites of every-day life. We also possess several volumes of the words of Buddha, consecrated to the great and indivisible Divine Being, and to all things that have come from his hands."

"Is there anything relating to the prophet Issa among these books?" I asked.

"No, sahib," returned the monk. "We have nothing but a few of the principal treatises relative to the observance of religious rites. As to the biographies of our saints, they are preserved at Lassa, and even some of the larger convents have not yet had time to procure copies of them.

Before coming here I lived many years in a large monastery at the other extremity of the Ladak, where I saw thousands of volumes and rolls of parchment copied at divers periods by the lamas of that place."

In the course of further conversation I learned that the convent in question was situated near Leh. My persistent inquiries, however, unfortunately aroused suspicion in the minds of the lamas, and it was with evident relief, on their part, that I was finally guided back to the inn; when, after a light supper, I soon fell into a sound sleep, leaving instructions to my Hindoo servant to cautiously ascertain — from the young lamas — the name of the convent in which their chief had lived before his appointment to Lamayure.

At daybreak I continued my journey, and, to my disappointment, learned from my servant that his efforts to gain information from the lamas had proved unsuccessful, as they were evidently on their guard.

I shall not pause here to speak of the convent life of these monks, for it is the same in all cloisters of the Ladak. I afterward visited the celebrated monastery of Leh, which I shall describe, in due time, giving full particulars concerning the curious existence led by the monks.

A steep declivity, running through a narrow gloomy defile that leads toward the Indus, begins at Lamayure.

Totally unconscious of the dangers lurking in the descent, I sent my carriers onward and encountered a passably good road stretching between two cliffs of brown argil. Soon, however, the path seemed to enter a narrow, obscure, subterranean passage, winding like a cornice along the rugged mountain side, above a precipice of frightful depth. A horseman, coming from the opposite direction, would assuredly have found it impossible to pass me on this overhanging shelf. Words are inadequate to describe the wild majestic beauty of this gorge, whose ridges tower loftily toward the heavens, lifting their crests proudly above the dark chasm beneath.

At some points the passage became so narrow that I could touch the opposite rocks with the tip of my cane from the saddle, while at times it seemed as if death was inevitable at every step. But it was now too late to alight from my horse, although I had never dreamed that I should soon find occasion to regret my foolish imprudence in entering this gorge alone. This passage, in fact, is nothing more than an enormous crevice formed by a powerful earthquake, which must have forcibly separated two gigantic masses of granite rocks. In the very depth of the defile is an impetuous torrent, whose loud roar fills the gorge with a mysterious murmur, though it seems but an almost invisible white thread; while above the traveler glimmers a narrow, winding, blue streak, which is the only part of the celestial arch revealed between the towering rocks. This majestic glimpse of nature inspired the most exquisite pleasure and delight, but the severe tranquillity, the frightful hush of the mountains, and the melancholy murmur of the torrent whose waters dashed against the granite rocks, filled me with unconquerable anguish. For a distance of nearly eight miles we were thus swayed between these sweet and painful sensations; then, after an abrupt turn to the right, our troop emerged into a small valley encircled with granite cliffs whose peaks are reflected in the Indus, and on the banks of which is found the small fortress of Khalsi. This celebrated fortress dates back to the time of the Mussulman invasions, and the only route from Kashmir to Thibet passes through it.

Having crossed the Indus on a semi-suspension bridge leading to the door of the fortress, which it is impossible to evade, I traversed the valley and the village of Khalsi, directing my steps toward the hamlet of Snourly, which is situated along the stream and built on terraces bordering the Indus, intending to spend the night there. The next two days I traveled quietly, and without encountering any difficulties, along the banks of the Indus, through a picturesque country that led me toward Leh, the capital of the Ladak.

Through the small valley of Saspoula, and over a territory of several kilometers surrounding the village of the same name, we saw a number of t'hortènes and shrines, and also two convents, over one of which floated the French flag. I afterward learned that a French engineer had made a present of it to the monks, who used it for decorative purposes.

I spent the night at Saspoula, and did not fail to visit the convent, the reader may rest assured. There, for the tenth time, I saw the eternal and dusty idols of Buddha, banners and flags piled into a corner, ugly masks littered over the floor, books and rolls of paper scattered in disorder, and a numberless quantity of prayer-wheels. The lamas take particular pleasure in making this exhibition, displaying the treasures of their convents with great pomp and pride, without in the least heeding the indifference or lack of interest natural to a stranger. "Everything must be shown, in the hope that the mere sight of these sacred objects may force the traveler to believe in the divine grandeur of the human soul."

As to the prophet Issa, they only repeated what I already knew — that the books which could give me any information concerning him were to be found at Lassa, and that the larger monasteries only possessed a few copies of them. I now abandoned all thought of going through the Karakorum, and determined to find the history of the prophet Issa, which would, perhaps, place the private life of the best of men under a new light and complete the vague accounts given of him in the New Testament.

At a short distance from Leh, and at the opening of the valley bearing the same name, the road stops short near an isolated rock, on the top of which stands a fort flanked with two towers and without garrison, and a small convent called Pitak. A mountain ten thousand five hundred feet in height protects the entrance of Thibet. The road then turns abruptly to the north in the direction of Leh, which is situated at an altitude of eleven thousand five hundred feet, six miles from Pitak, and at the base of immense granitic columns, with pinnacles enshrouded in eternal snows rising to an elevation of eighteen thousand to nineteen thousand feet. The city itself is encircled by a belt of stunted aspen-trees, and is elevated on successive terraces, dominated by an old fort and the palace of the ancient sovereigns of the Ladak. At twilight I reached Leh, and descended into a bungalow especially constructed for Europeans who come over the Indian route in the hunting season.

THE LADAK.

THE Ladak formerly made part of Great Thibet. But the frequent invasions of northern nations, who traversed this country in attempting to conquer Kashmir, and the many wars of which it was the scene of action, not only reduced it to misery, but also resulted in its separation from the political domination of Lassa by its passing from the hands of one conqueror to those of another. The Mohammedans, who took possession of Kashmir and the Ladak at an early period, forcibly converted the weak inhabitants of Little Thibet to Islamism. The political existence of the Ladak ended with the annexation of that country to Kashmir by the Sikhs, when the people were permitted to again practice their ancient religion. Two-thirds of the inhabitants took advantage of this freedom to reconstruct their gonpas and resumed their former life; the Baltistans alone remaining Schiit-Mussulmans, a sect to which the conquerors of the country had belonged. Notwithstanding this, however, they have retained but a very vague tinge of Islamism;

the character of which is revealed mostly in their customs and the polygamy they practice. The lamas declare that they do not yet despair of bringing them back to the faith of their ancestors

In regard to religion the Ladak is dependent on Lassa, the capital of Thibet and the residence of the Dalaï-Lama; it is at Lassa also that the principal Khutuktus, or supreme lamas, and the Chogzots, or managers, are elected. Politically it is under the authority of the Maharaja of Kashmir, who appoints the governor.

The population of the Ladak is essentially Mongolian, but is divided into Ladakians and Tchampas. They lead a sedentary life, build villages along the narrow valleys, dwell in neat two-story houses, and cultivate a few patches of land. They are excessively ill-favored, being of small stature, hollow-cheeked, and round-shouldered, with a small head, narrow receding forehead, the bright dark eyes of the Mongolian race, a flat nose, a large mouth and thin lips, and a short chin, adorned with a sparse beard, in which ends the net of wrinkles that furrow the two hollow cheeks. Such is the Ladakian. To this add a shaven head, from which hangs a very slender braid of hair, and you have not only the general type of the inhabitants of Ladak, but of the entire Thibet.

The women are also of small stature, and possess prominent cheek-bones; but they are of more robust constitution and the roses bloom in their cheeks, while a sympathetic smile continually hovers about their lips. They are gentle in disposition and exceedingly gay, being very fond of laughter.

The severity of the climate and the rugged nature of the country deprive the people of rich clothing of varied colors. Their shirts are of common unbleached linen and of rough cloth of home manufacture; while their trousers, of the same material, are made to reach the knee. Men of means add a choga (coat) to this. A fur cap, with earlaps, is worn in the winter; while a cloth cap with a side flap does duty in the summer. A whole arsenal of small objects hang from their belts; among which may be found a case of needles, a knife, a pen and inkstand, a tobacco pouch, and the inevitable prayer-wheel.

Male Thibetans, as a rule, are so intensely indolent, that when their hair becomes loosened, it remains unbraided for three months; and once they have put on a shirt, it is worn until it falls in tatters from their bodies. Their coats are always dirty, and invariably bear the stamp of their braid of hair, which they never forget to grease carefully every day. They wash their faces once a year; not of their own free will, but because constrained by the law. The stench they spread around them is, in fact, so intense that strangers approach them only when absolutely necessary.

The women, on the contrary, are exceedingly fond of order and cleanliness; bathing constantly every day, and upon any excuse. A red gown is worn over their dazzling white and well-molded shoulders, confined below the waist within narrow red and green pantaloons, over which falls a wide cloth skirt elaborately plaited. A pair of red shoes, embroidered and lined with fur, completes this house costume. The hair is worn in a thin braid, to which is pinned a large piece of loose cloth somewhat resembling the Italian headdress; beneath this peculiar veil is suspended a variety of bright colored pebbles, coins, and fragments of carved metals; the ears are covered with two tongues of cloth or fur; and a lined lamb-skin is worn over the shoulders, barely covering the back. While the poor are satisfied with a plain fur skin, for outdoor wear, the women of wealth wear a veritable pelisse, trimmed with red cloth and gold fringe.

Whether merely strolling through the streets or calling on their neighbors, these women invariably carry on their backs a basket of conical shape, in which they gather their fuel from the dunghills. Every woman possesses money of her own, which she invariably spends on trinkets; usually buying large pieces of turquoise, which are cheap enough, and adding them to the odd ornaments of her head-dress. I have seen stones of this kind that weighed fully five pounds.

The Ladakian woman holds a social position envied by all her Oriental sisters, for she is free and respected; and, save for the few hours of light work she does in the fields, spends nearly all her time in exchanging neighborly visits, although it must be here remarked that "gossiping" is unknown.

Agriculture is the general occupation of the fixed population of the Ladak; but the inhabitants possess so little land — the portion of each being about ten acres — that the income derived therefrom barely suffices for the mere necessaries of life, leaving nothing toward the payment of taxes. Trades are generally despised; and laborers and musicians, who compose the lowest degree of society, are known under the contemptuous name of Bem, and universally shunned. The hours of leisure left, after their work in the fields is accomplished, is spent in hunting the Thibet goat, whose fur is greatly valued in India; while the poorer inhabitants, who can not afford the necessary weapons, hire themselves as coolies. This sport is also engaged in by women, whose powers of endurance are remarkable, and who really bear the hardships encountered in the chase much better than their husbands, the latter being so intensely lazy that they are quite capable of spending the whole night out of doors, lying on a stone, indifferent alike to heat and cold.

Polyandry (a subject which later on I shall return to more in detail) has the effect of uniting the people more closely, by forming large families who till their land in common, with their yaks, zos, and zomos (oxen and cows). No member of a family can at any time leave it; and when one dies, his share reverts to the community.

Wheat is the principal crop, but, owing to the harshness of the climate, the grain is exceedingly small. Barley is also cultivated, and is pulverized before being sold. When the harvest is over, the men repair to the mountains to gather a wild plant called "Enoriota" and a species of tall thistle, or "dama," which are used for fuel, wood being extremely scarce in the Ladak. Forests and gardens are unknown, and it is only at rare intervals that sickly clumps of poplars and willows are found on the banks of the streams. A few aspens may also be sometimes seen near the villages; but for lack of fertile soil gardening can not thrive.

The scarcity of wood is particularly noticeable in the buildings, which are constructed of sun-dried bricks, or of medium-sized stones, cemented together with a sort of mortar composed of argil and chopped straw.

The houses of the sedentary Ladakians consist of two stories, with carefully white-washed walls and brightly-painted windows, the horizontal roofs forming terraces which are decked with wild flowers, and where, during the fine season, the inmates kill time contemplating nature and keeping their prayer-wheels in motion. Each of these dwellings contains several rooms, all furnished with a bed and other articles of furniture, save one, which is reserved for visitors and hung with the most beautiful skins. In the homes of the wealthier class, there is also an apartment specially devoted to prayer and filled with idols.

A most regular existence is led here. Everything is eaten without much choice, but the principal food is of the plainest kind. Breakfast consists of a morsel of rye bread; while at noon a bowl of flour is placed on the table, warm water poured into it, and the whole stirred with small sticks until it attains the consistency of a thick batter, which is then rolled into small balls and eaten with milk; for supper, bread and tea are served. Meat is a superfluous luxury, little used save by hunters who introduce a certain degree of variety in their meals by eating the flesh of wild goats, eagles, or white pheasants, which are quite plentiful in this country.

A great quantity of tchang, a sort of pale unfermented beer, is drunk all day long.

Should a Ladakian leave home, in search of work in a neighboring village, on a pony — and these privileged beings are few indeed — he invariably provides himself with a small quantity of flour for the journey. The dinner hour having arrived, he seeks a river or spring, mixes a little flour and water together in a wooden cup which he always carries, and sits quietly down to enjoy his meal.

The Tchampas, or nomads, who compose the other portion of the population of the Ladak, are much poorer and coarser than the sedentary Ladakians. They are mostly hunters, and neglect agriculture completely. Although professing the Buddhist religion, they never enter a monastery unless in need of flour, which they obtain in exchange for game; and their favorite dwelling place is a tent on the summit of the mountains, where the cold is excessive. While the Ladakians, properly speaking, are anxious to gain knowledge, proverbially indolent and truthful, the Tchampas, on the contrary, are irritable, extremely active, inveterate liars, and profess utter contempt for convents. Dwelling among them is the little colony of the Khomba, a bohemian set of people who came from the vicinity of Lassa, and lead a miserable existence as mendicants. Incapable of work, and speaking a tongue not understood in the country in which they beg their bread, they are objects of universal scorn, being tolerated only through compassion for their deplorable condition when starvation drives them in numbers into the villages.

Polyandry, which is practiced in all families, deeply aroused my curiosity. It is by no means a consequence attending the doctrines of Buddhism, for this custom existed long before the appearance of Buddha. It has assumed enormous proportions in India, where it constitutes one of the most active means of checking a population that ever tends to increase; and even at the present day, the practice of killing female children at birth makes terrible ravages in that country; all efforts on the part of the English having proved fruitless in their struggle against the suppression of future mothers. Manou himself made polyandry a law, and Buddhist preachers, who had abjured Brahmanism and advocated the use of opium, imported the custom into the island of Ceylon, Thibet, Mongolia, and Korea. Though long suppressed in China, polyandry, whose stronghold is in Thibet and Ceylon, also flourishes among the Kalmuks, between Todas in Southern India, and Nairs on the Malabar Coast. Traces of this odd marriage constitution are also found among the Tasmanians, and in North America among the Iroquois.

Furthermore, polyandry has even flourished in Europe, if we are to believe Cæsar, who says in his "De Bello Gallico." liv. V, page 17: "*Uxores habent deni duodenique inter se communes, et maximè fratres cum fratribus et parentes cum liberis.*"

All this proves conclusively that it is impossible to look upon polyandry as a religious custom. In Thibet, it may be explained by motives of an economic order, if we take into consideration the average quantity of tillable land falling to each of its inhabitants. To maintain a population of one million five hundred thousand on a surface of one million two hundred thousand square kilometers, the Buddhists were forced to adopt polyandry, while each family is moreover obliged to furnish one member to a religious order. The first-born son is pledged to a gonpa, which is invariably found on one of the heights near each village. When the child has attained the age of eight years, he is intrusted to a caravan on its way to Lassa, where he enters one of the convents and remains until the age of fifteen as a novice. There he learns to read and write, and studies the religious rites and the sacred parchments written in the Pali tongue, the language formerly spoken in the Maguada Country, where, according to tradition, Buddha Gautama was born.

The elder brother chooses a wife who becomes the common property of every member of his family. The choice of the bride and the nuptial ceremony are both accomplished in the most primitive way. When a woman and her several husbands decide upon the marriage of one of their sons, the elder brother is sent to pay a visit to a neighbor with a marriageable daughter.

The first and second visits are spent in commonplace conversation, intermingled with frequent libations of tchang; and it is only on the occasion of his third visit that the young man announces his intention of taking upon himself a wife. The young girl, who is not unknown to the prospective groom, since the women of Ladak never veil their faces, is then brought forward.

A young girl can not be married without her consent; but if she accepts the proposal, the young man takes her with him to his home, where she becomes his wife and that of his brothers. A family with but one son, sends him to a woman who has two or three husbands only, and he offers himself in the role of third or fourth husband. This offer is not usually declined, and the young man immediately takes his place in the bosom of his new family.

Children are sometimes also married at a very tender age; but they always remain in their respective families until they have attained, or even passed, a marriageable age. Should a young girl give birth to a child before marriage, she is not only shielded from public scorn, but is, on the contrary, surrounded with every mark of the greatest respect; for she is prolific, and a host of men rival the favor of her hand. A woman has the right to have an unlimited number of husbands or lovers. In the latter case, she invites the young man of her choice into her home, and quietly announces that she has taken a new lover "jing-tuh;" a piece of information received with perfect equanimity on the part of the discarded husbands, and even with joy when the wife of their bosoms has proved barren in the first three years of her marriage.

Jealousy is unknown. The Thibetan is of too cold a temperament to understand love; which, for him, would almost seem an anachronism, even if it were not a flagrant violation of the custom which makes women common to all; in a word, to his eyes, love would appear a luxury that nothing could justify.

In the absence of one of the husbands, his place is offered to a bachelor or a widower — although the latter are in great minority, the wife usually surviving her debilitated husbands — or a Buddhist traveler, whose business may retain him for some time in the village, is sometimes chosen instead. A married man who travels, or finds himself in a neighboring town in search of work, always takes advantage of the hospitality of his co-religionists, who place their own wives at his disposal as well as their roofs; and in case a woman has remained sterile, the husbands are really importunate in their offers, hoping thereby to become fathers.

Notwithstanding her peculiar position, the woman is entirely free in the choice of a husband or lover; she enjoys the esteem and respect of all, is always cheerful, takes part in everything that is discussed, and goes unimpeded wherever she pleases, save in the principal chamber of prayers in the monastery, the entrance of which is formally interdicted to her.

The children recognize their mother only, and feel no affection for their fathers for the excellent reason that they possess an infinity of them. Although I do not approve of polyandry, I can scarcely condemn its practice in Thibet. Were it not for it, the population would increase prodigiously; famines and misery would spread over the whole nation with their entire sinister train,— murder, theft, etc., crimes which are yet absolutely unknown in that entire country.

A FEAST IN A GONPA.

LEH, the capital of the Ladak, is a small town of five thousand inhabitants, with two or three streets bordered with neat white houses, and a market square, or bazaar, where the merchants of India, China, Turkestan, Kashmir, and Thibet come to exchange their products for Thibetan gold, brought by the natives, for the purchase of cloth garments for their monks, as well as for many articles of absolute necessity for themselves.

An old deserted palace stands on one of the hills that rises above the town; while in the very center of the town is a vast two-story building, in which resides the Governor of the Ladak, the Surajbal Vizier — a most intelligent and able ruler, who obtained his degree of philosophy in London.

To celebrate my visit in Leh, the Governor organized a polo game on the square — this game, introduced by the English, having become the national game of the Thibetans — ending the evening with a round of dances and games in

A FEAST IN A GONPA.

front of his own terrace. A number of bonfires threw their red glares over the crowd of spectators who formed a circle around a group of personages disguised as animals, devils, and witches; leaping, skipping, and twirling, and executing strange dances measured by the monotonous music of two straight trumpets, accompanied by a drum. The infernal racket produced by these instruments, added to the continual hue and cry of the crowd, wearied me so intensely that it finally became well-nigh unendurable.

The ceremony terminated with the graceful dances of the women, who twirled on their heels, swayed to and fro, courtesied beneath our windows, and gaily jingled their bracelets of ivory and brass by crossing their hands near the wrists.

I rose early the following morning and started in the direction of a large convent called Ifimis, which stands on a most picturesque site at the summit of a high rock rising in the middle of a valley that dominates the Indus. It is one of the principal monasteries of the country, and is supported by gifts from the inhabitants and subsidies sent from Lassa. On the road to the convent, after having crossed the Indus and a number of small villages, we found innumerable shrines with stones covered with inscriptions, as well as many t'hortènes which our guides carefully passed on the right side. Once I tried to turn my horse to the left, but the Ladakians made me turn back, leading my steed by the bridle, and explaining that it was customary to turn to the right. I found it impossible, however, to learn the origin of this custom.

We wended our way on foot toward the gonpa, which is surmounted by an embattled tower visible from afar, and soon found ourselves before a large, brightly-painted door, forming part of a vast building inclosing a graveled court. To the right, in one of the angles, is a large painted door adorned with big brass rings. This is the entrance to the principal temple, which is decorated with paintings of the chief idols and an immense statue of Buddha surrounded by a multitude of sacred statuettes. To the left is a verandah ornamented with a huge prayer-wheel, around which the lamas were gathered in a circle. Below and directly beneath this verandah were a few musicians with long trumpets and drums in their hands.

To the right of the court is a row of doors giving access to the rooms occupied by the monks, all decorated with sacred paintings and prayer-wheels, the latter surmounted by black and red tridents with floating ribbons covered with inscriptions.

emitted a shrill whistle. In response to this signal a band of young men in warrior's dress rushed out of the temple; they wore short shirts, with strings of sleigh-bells dangling around their limbs and tied with ribbons that fluttered in the breeze, while their heads were concealed beneath monstrous green masks, over which floated triangular red banners. With a diabolical din of tambourines and bells they began a whirling, dizzying dance around the gods that were seated on the ground, while two tall fellows in clownish tights executed a series of grotesque leaps and contortions that threw the spectators into spasms of laughter.

A new group, whose disguise consisted of red miters and yellow pantaloons, came out of the temple with bells and tambourines and took up the space opposite the gods, this representing the greatest power next to divinity.

Then more red and brown masked figures with three eyes painted on their breasts appeared on the scene. Two rows of dancers were now formed and a general dance followed, the masked men marching forward and backward, turning in a circle here and forming into columns there, only pausing long enough now and then to bow to the audience and form into new figures.

This monotonous performance finally came to

the main entrance, where they ranged themselves on the stairway.

An instant of complete silence followed, at the end of which we saw a third group of disguised men emerge from the temple, their enormous masks representing different deities and bearing a third eye on their foreheads.

Marching at the head was Thlogan-Poudma-Jungnas, signifying "born in the lotus flower." He was accompanied by another masked personage, richly dressed and carrying a large yellow parasol covered with drawings. His suite was composed of gods in magnificent costume: Dorje-Trolong, Sangspa-Kourpo (Brahma), and others. These masks, as the lama nearest to us explained, represented six classes of beings subject to metamorphosis-gods, demi-gods, men, animals, spirits, and demons.

On each side of these personages, advancing so gravely, walked other masked men in silk garments of dazzling colors, with tessellated gold crown bordered with six gems and surmounted by a long arrow, and each carrying a drum.

In this order and amid the din of clashing, incoherent music, they marched thrice around the tall poles, then sat on the ground in a circle about Thlogan-Poudma-Jungnas, the three-eyed-god, who gravely stuck two fingers in his mouth and a peculiar sort of spoon made of the fragment of a human skull bound with a piece of ribbon, to which was attached a tuft of hair torn — it was claimed — from the scalps of their enemies. Their promenade around the poles soon developed into a sort of wild dance, which was brought to a sudden stop by a more emphasized bang on the drum, only to recommence a moment later, the dancers now wielding yellow sticks decked with ribbons, which they held in a menacing attitude in their right hands. They then advanced and saluted the chief lama, after which they stationed themselves near the door leading to the temple.

At this same moment other personages, with heads incased in brass masks, emerged from the principal doors of the temple. They were clothed in embroidered robes of different hues and carried a small tambourine in one hand, while with the other they jingled a string of small bells. A drum-stick hung against each tambourine, and the slightest movement of the hand brought it in contact with the sonorous vellum, producing a strange sound. These new dancers marched around the court several times, accompanying their steps with a soft beating of the tambourines. After each round there was a pause, then a terrible din, produced by a tremendous beating of the tambourines in unison, after which all ran toward

A FEAST IN A GONPA. 79

In the center of the court are two tall poles, from the tips of which float yak-tails and narrow paper streamers bearing religious precepts. Along the walls of the convent are more prayer-wheels ornamented with ribbons.

A profound silence reigned in the court; all were anxiously awaiting the representation of a religious mystery about to begin. We took our places on the verandah, not far from the lamas, and almost immediately the musicians intoned a soft monotonous melody on their trumpets, to the accompaniment of a queer looking drum supported on a stick planted into the ground.

At the first notes of the melancholy chant that accompanied this fantastic music, the doors along the convent wall opened to admit a procession of a score of personages disguised as animals, birds, devils, and inconceivable monsters. On their breasts were fantastic dragons, demons, and skulls, embroidered in Chinese silk of different hues. Their head-dress consisted of a conical-shaped hat, with long multi-colored ribbons falling over the breast and elaborately inscribed; while over the face was worn a mask representing a skull, embroidered in white silk. Thus appareled, they slowly circled around the tall poles standing in the middle of the court, waving their arms and brandishing from their left hands

A FEAST IN A GONPA.

an end, and gods, demi-gods, kings, men, and spirits rose, and, followed by the masked forms, solemnly marched toward the principal door of the temple, from which came another group disguised as skeletons. Each of these movements had its particular signification and was carefully calculated beforehand. The advancing throng paused and made way for this procession of skeletons, who gravely, and with measured steps, marched to the tall poles, where they stopped and shook the wooden clappers that hung to their sides, producing a noise resembling the snapping of the jaws. They then walked twice around the court, keeping step to the music of the tambourines, and finally intoned a religious chant. After more snapping of their artificial jaws and grinding of teeth — imitated to perfection — they executed a few difficult feats, in which the contortions were really painful to witness, and came to a rest at last.

The image of the "enemy of men," made of dough and placed at the foot of one of the poles, was then seized upon and broken, and the pieces distributed among the skeletons by the old men who stood among the spectators, this signifying — so it seems — that they were holding themselves in readiness to soon join them in the cemetery.

The chief lama now approached me and extended a polite invitation to accompany him to the principal terrace and drink the tchang of the feast, an offer which I accepted with pleasure, the performance I had just witnessed having made me rather dizzy.

Having crossed the court and ascended a stairway encumbered by prayer-wheels, we passed through two rooms, in which were numberless images of gods, and stepped out on the terrace, where I seated myself on a bench facing the venerable lama, whose eyes sparkled with intelligence.

Three lamas immediately brought jugs of tchang, which they poured into small brass cups, serving the chief lama first, then myself and servants.

"Did you enjoy our little celebration?" inquired the lama.

"It was very fine," I answered, " and I have not yet been able to shake off the impression made on me by the spectacle I have just witnessed. But, I must admit, that I never imagined for a moment that Buddhism could surround its religious ceremonies with so gaudy, not to say clamorous, exterior forms."

"There is no religion in which the ceremonies assume a more theatrical form," returned the lama. "It is a ritual part of the service which

A FEAST IN A GONPA. 85

in no way violates the fundamental principles of Buddhism, being merely a practical means of maintaining the ignorant throng in the obedience and love of the Creator, as a toy may keep a child under the submission of his parents. The people, or the ignorant throng, are the children of the Father."

"But what is the meaning of all those masks, costumes, bells, dances, and, in a general way, of this entire performance, which seems to be executed from a fixed programme?" I asked.

"We have many such feasts in the year," replied the lama, "and we invite outsiders to represent the mysteries, which bear a strong analogy to pantomimes, and in which each actor may execute almost any figure or movement he chooses, provided he conforms himself to the circumstances and keeps the main idea in view. Our mysteries are nothing more than pantomimes, which should represent the gods as enjoying universal veneration; a veneration that should be rewarded by that cheerfulness of soul which comes from the simultaneous knowledge of inevitable death and of a future existence. The actors wear garments belonging to the gonpa, and act according to general instructions, which leave them full freedom of gesture. The effect produced is undoubtedly magnificent, but the spectators must guess the signification of each part for themselves. You sometimes also have recourse to this expedient, which in no way affects the principle of monotheism itself."

"Excuse my interruption," I broke in, "but that mass of idols which encumbers your gonpas is certainly a gross violation of this principle!"

"As I have already said," explained the lama, "man is, and always will be, in his infancy. He understands, sees, and feels the grandeur of nature, but he neither sees nor understands the great spirit which has created and animated all things. Man has always sought tangible things, it being impossible for him to believe long in what escapes his material senses. He has racked his brains to find the means of contemplating the Creator, trying to enter into direct relations with the Supreme Being who has given him so many blessings, and, as he erroneously believes, many unnecessary trials too. This explains why he began to worship those parts of nature from which he received benefits. We see a striking example of this in the ancient Egyptians, who worshiped animals, trees, and stones, winds and tempests. Other nations, steeped more deeply in ignorance, seeing that the results of winds were not always favorable, that rain was not infallible in producing good crops, and that animals fre-

A FEAST IN A GONPA.

quently disobeyed the will of man, sought a direct intermediary between themselves and the great unfathomable and mysterious power of the Creator. Thus they created idols, which they regarded as neutral to all their surroundings, and to whose mediation they always had recourse. From the remotest periods to the present day, man has never known any tendency but toward tangible reality. In seeking a path that might lead them to the feet of the Creator, the Assyrians turned their gaze toward the planets, which they contemplated but could not reach. This belief the Guebers retain to this day. In their nullity and blindness of mind, men are incapable of conceiving the invisible and spiritual link that unites them to the great Divinity, which explains why they have sought palpable things existing within the domain of the senses; thus aiming an attenuating blow at the divine principle. However, they have never dared attribute a divine and eternal existence to the visible images which are their own handwork. The same fact may be observed in Brahmanism, where men, who have been left to their inclination in regard to exterior forms, have gradually — and not in one day — created an army of gods and demi-gods. The Israelites have probably demonstrated in the most conclusive manner the inherent love of man for all that is concrete; notwithstanding a series of dazzling miracles performed by the great Creator, who is the same for all nations, the people of Israel could not help setting up a god cast in metal, at the very moment when their prophet Mossa was conversing with the Creator!

"Buddhism has undergone the same modifications. Our great reformer, Cakya-Mouni, who was inspired by the Supreme Judge, truly understood the one and indivisible majesty of Brahma, and did all in his power to prevent the manufacture of images, made, it was claimed, in his resemblance; he openly separated himself from the polytheistic Brahmans and preached the purity and immortality of Brahma. The success obtained by himself and his disciples among the people caused him to be persecuted by the Brahmans, who had acquired a source of personal revenue in creating new gods, and who, contrary to the law of God, treated the nation despotically. Our first sacred preachers, whom we call Buddhas, which means learned and saintly, because the Great Creator incarnated himself in them, dwelt in different parts of the world. As their sermons were mainly directed against the tyranny of the Brahmans and their profitable business in propagating this idea of God, the Buddhists — that is

A FEAST IN A GONPA.   89

those who have followed the doctrine of these holy preachers — were mostly gathered from the lower classes of China and India. Among these sacred preachers, the Buddha, Cakya-Mouni, known in China under the name of Fô, who lived three thousand years ago and whose sermons brought the whole of China back into the path of the true God, and the Buddha Gautama, who lived two thousand five-hundred years ago and converted nearly half of the Hindoos to the word of the only invisible and impersonal God, are particularly venerated.

"Buddhism is divided into many sects, which differ only in some of the religious ceremonies, the basis of the doctrine being the same in all. The Thibetan Buddhists, whom we call Lamaists, separated from the Foists fifteen hundred years ago. Until then we had formed part of the worshipers of the Buddha Fô Cakya-Mouni, who was the first to unite all the laws enacted by the different Buddhas at the time of the great schism among the Brahmans. Later, a Mongolian, Khutuktus, translated the works of the great Buddha into Chinese, for which the Emperor of China rewarded him with the title of Go-Chi — King's preceptor. After his death this title was bestowed on the Dalaï-Lama of Thibet, and since that epoch the incumbent of this post has enjoyed the dignified name of Go-Chi—in fact, our religion itself is called Lamaism (Superior). Red monks and yellow monks are admitted. The former marry and recognize the authority of the Bantsin, who resides at Techow-Lumba and is chief of the civil administration of Thibet; we yellow lamas take vows of celibacy, and our direct chief is the Dalaï-Lama. This constitutes the difference between these two religious orders, whose ritual is identical."

"Do they all organize such mysteries as I have just witnessed?"

"Yes, with few exceptions. These feasts were formerly celebrated with solemn pomp, but our gonpas have been repeatedly pillaged and our riches stolen since the conquest of the Ladak, and we must now be satisfied with white garments and bronze utensils, while in Thibet nothing is seen but gold embroidery and gold vessels."

"In a recent visit to one of your gonpas a lama spoke to me of a prophet, or, as you perhaps call him, a Buddha of the name of Issa. Can you tell me anything of him?" I asked, grasping the first favorable opportunity of broaching the subject that was of paramount interest to me.

"The name of Issa is greatly respected among the Buddhists," was the reply, "though little is known of him save by the chief lamas who have

A FEAST IN A GONPA.

read the parchments relating to his life. We have an unlimited number of Buddhas, such as Issa, and the eighty-four thousand rolls of parchment in existence are replete with details of them all; but few men have read the one-hundredth part of these records. In conformity with an established custom, no pupil or lama who visits Lassa fails to present one or several copies of these to the convent to which he belongs; our gonpa, being among the fortunate ones, already possesses a large number of manuscripts, which I read in my leisure hours. Among these copies I have found descriptions of the life and deeds of Issa, who preached in India and among the sons of Israel, and who was afterward put to death by pagans whose descendants adopted the doctrine he taught, the doctrine in which you believe. The Great Buddha, soul of the universe, is the incarnation of Brahma; he remains inert nearly always, containing all things within him since the origin of man, and his breath animates the world. He abandoned man to his own strength; yet, at certain epochs, he emerges from his inaction and assumes a human form, that he may attempt to snatch his creatures from irremediable ruin. In the course of his terrestrial existence, Buddha creates a new world in the midst of the people who have gone astray, then leaves this earth to again become an invisible being and resume his life of perfect felicity.

"Three thousand years ago the Great Buddha incarnated himself in the person of the celebrated prince, Cakya-Mouni, by maintaining and propagating the doctrines of his twenty incarnations. Two thousand five hundred years ago the great soul of the world incarnated himself once more in Gautama, building the foundations of a new world in Burma, Siam, and different islands. Shortly afterward, thanks to the perseverance of the wise men who applied themselves to the propagation of the holy doctrine, Buddhism began to penetrate into China; and about the year 2050, under Ming-Ti, of the Honi dynasty, the doctrine of Cakya-Mouni was finally adopted by the people. Simultaneously with the apparition of Buddhism in China, the doctrine began to spread among the Israelites. And about two thousand years ago the perfect Being, arousing again from his inaction for a period, incarnated himself into the newborn child of a poor family; he willed that infant lips, by employing popular images, might enlighten unfortunate humanity on the life beyond the grave, and, by his own example, bring back men to the true way and into the path that might best lead them to original moral purity. When the sacred child had attained a certain age, he was

A FEAST IN A GONPA.

taken to India, where, until he attained manhood, he studied the laws of the Great Buddha who resides eternally in heaven."

"In what tongue are written the principal rolls relative to the life of Issa?" I asked, rising, for my interesting companion was beginning to show signs of fatigue, and had set a small prayer-wheel in motion to put an end to the conversation.

"The rolls which treat of the life of Issa, and which were brought from India to Nepal, and from Nepal to Thibet, are written in the Pali tongue, and are now at Lassa; but we possess one copy in our own tongue; that is in the Thibetan language."

"How is Issa looked upon in Thibet? Does he bear the reputation of a saint?"

"The people ignore his very existence; the great lamas, who have studied the parchments relating to his life, alone know of him. But as his doctrine does not constitute a canonical part of Buddhism, and the worshipers of Issa do not acknowledge the authority of the Dalaï-Lama, this prophet — like many of his kind — is not recognized as one of the principal saints in Thibet."

"Would you be committing a sin, if you were to read these copies to a stranger?" I queried.

"What belongs to God," he replied, "belongs

also to men. It is our duty to cheerfully assist in the propagation of his doctrine; but I do not know where these papers are to be found. Should you ever again visit our gonpa, however, I will show them to you with pleasure."

We were interrupted at this juncture by the entrance of two monks, who said a few words — unintelligible to me — and hastily retired.

"I am summoned to attend the sacrifices. Pray excuse me," said the lama, with a bow, as he moved toward the door.

Nothing remained for me to do but to retire to the chamber allotted to my use; where I sought my bed, after partaking of food and milk, and slept soundly till morning.

The next night I was back at Leh, racking my brains to invent a pretext to again visit the convent.

Two days later I dispatched a messenger with an alarm clock, a watch, and a thermometer, as gifts to the chief lama, with the information that, before leaving the Ladak, I would probably return to the convent, in the hope that he would not refuse to let me see the book which had formed the subject of our conversation.

My intention was to go to Kashmir, and return to Himis sometime later, but fate decided otherwise. While passing along the foot of the

A FEAST IN A GONPA. 95

mountain, on which is perched the gonpa Piatak, my horse stumbled, throwing me violently to the ground and breaking my leg above the knee. It was now impossible to continue my journey; and as I had no desire to return to Leh, and the prospect of begging the hospitality of the gonpa, which is a mere hovel, was anything but enchanting, I ordered my servants to take me to Himis, which was only a half-day's journey. After much intense suffering, my leg was finally bandaged, and I was hoisted into the saddle. With one man supporting my injured limb and another leading my horse by the bridle, we started slowly back, reaching Himis at a late hour of the night.

On hearing of the accident that had befallen me, the monks immediately rushed out to receive me. With infinite precautions I was borne to their best chamber and deposited on a mountain of soft bedding, with a prayer-wheel placed at my side. All this was done under the direct supervision of their chief, who affectionately pressed my hand when I stretched it out to thank him for his kindness.

The succeeding morning 1 incased the injured member in thin boards held together with strings, and did my best to remain motionless. A favorable result was soon apparent, and two days later I was well enough to undertake a slow journey toward India, in quest of a physician.

While a young man kept the prayer-wheel in motion by my bedside, the venerable director of the gonpa entertained me with interesting accounts of their belief and the country in general, meanwhile frequently pulling out the watch and alarm clock, and interrupting his discourse to question me in regard to their use and the manner of winding them both. Finally, yielding to my earnest solicitations, he brought forth two big volumes in cardboard covers, with leaves yellowed by the lapse of time, and read the biography of Issa, which I carefully copied from the translation of my interpreter. This curious document is written in the form of isolated verses, which frequently bear no connection between each other.

On the third day my condition was favorable enough to permit me to continue my journey, and I again started for India by way of Kashmir. Twenty long days of excruciating suffering were spent on the way; but by means of a letter kindly sent me by Monsieur Peicheau, a Frenchman—whom I now take the opportunity of thanking for his courteous hospitality—and with an order from the grand-vizier of the Maharaja of Kashmir to the authorities to furnish me with bearers, I finally reached Serinagur, which I almost immediately left again as I was anxious to arrive in India before the first snowfall.

A FEAST IN A GONPA.

At Murree I met another kind Frenchman, Count André de Saint-Phall, who was taking a pleasure trip through Hindoostan. Throughout the whole journey we made together to Bombay, during which I suffered intolerable pain from my broken leg and the consequent fever, the young count showed himself full of the most tender solicitude for me. My heart is still filled with sincere gratitude toward him; and neither shall I ever forget the friendly attentions showered upon me on my arrival in Bombay by the Marquis de Mores, the Viscount de Breteuil, Monsieur Monod of the Comptoir d'Escompte, Monsieur Moet, consul, and all the Frenchmen of that sympathetic French colony.

I have long cherished the project of publishing the memoirs on the life of Jesus Christ, which I found at Himis, and of which I have already spoken; but affairs of all sorts have completely absorbed my time until this day. It is only after many sleepless nights spent in the classification of all my notes, after grouping the verses in conformity with the course of the narrative, and imprinting a character of unity to the entire work, that I now finally consent to give publication to the curious manuscript that follows.

THE LIFE OF SAINT ISSA.

THE BEST OF THE SONS OF MEN.

I.

1. The earth has trembled and the heavens have wept, because of the great crime just committed in the land of Israel.

2. For they have put to torture and executed the great just Issa, in whom dwelt the spirit of the world.

3. Which was incarnated in a simple mortal, that men might be benefited and evil thoughts exterminated thereby.

4. And that it might bring back to a life of peace, of love, and happiness, man degraded by sin, and recall to him the only and indivisible Creator whose mercy is boundless and infinite.

THE LIFE OF SAINT ISSA.

5. This is what is related on this subject by the merchants who have come from Israel.

II.

1. The people of Israel, who inhabited a most fertile land, yielding two crops a year, and who possessed immense flocks, excited the wrath of God through their sins.

2. And he inflicted upon them a terrible punishment by taking away their land, their flocks, and all they possessed; and Israel was reduced to slavery by the rich and powerful Pharaohs who then reigned in Egypt.

3. The latter treated the Israelites more cruelly than animals, loading them with chains and putting them to the roughest labor; they covered their bodies with bruises and wounds, and denied them food and shelter,

4. That they might be kept in a state of continual terror and robbed of all semblance of humanity;

100 UNKNOWN LIFE OF CHRIST.

5. And in their dire distress, the children of Israel, remembering their heavenly protector, addressed their prayers to him and implored his assistance and mercy.

6. An illustrious Pharaoh then reigned in Egypt, who had become celebrated for his numerous victories, the great riches he had amassed, and the vast palaces which his slaves had erected with their own hands.

7. This Pharaoh had two sons, the younger of whom was called Mossa; and the learned Israelites taught him divers sciences.

8. And Mossa was beloved throughout the land of Egypt for his goodness and the compassion he displayed for them that suffered.

9. Seeing that, notwithstanding the intolerable sufferings they endured, the Israelites refused to abandon their God to worship those created by the hands of man and which were the gods of the Egyptians.

10. Mossa believed in their indivisible God,

THE LIFE OF SAINT ISSA. 101

who did not allow their flagging strength to falter.

11. And the Israelite preceptors encouraged Mossa's ardor and had recourse to him, begging him to intercede with Pharaoh, his father, in favor of his co-religionists.

12. Prince Mossa pleaded with his father to soften the lot of these unhappy people, but Pharaoh became angry with him and only imposed more hardships upon his slaves.

13. It came to pass, not long after, that a great calamity fell upon Egypt; the plague decimated the young and the old, the strong and the sick; and Pharaoh believed he had incurred the wrath of his own gods against him;

14. But the prince Mossa declared to his father, that it was the God of his slaves who was interfering in favor of his unhappy people and punishing the Egyptians;

15. Pharaoh commanded Mossa, his son, to gather all the slaves of Jewish race, to lead them

away to a great distance from the capital and found another city, where he should remain with them.

16. Mossa announced to the Hebrew slaves that he had delivered them in the name of their God, the God of Israel; and he went with them out of the city and of the land of Egypt.

17. He therefore led them into the land they had lost through their many sins; he gave them laws and enjoined them to always pray to the invisible Creator whose goodness is infinite.

18. At the death of the prince Mossa, the Israelites rigorously observed his laws, and God recompensed them for the wrongs they had suffered in Egypt.

19. Their kingdom became the most powerful in all the world, their kings gained renown for their treasures, and a long period of peace prevailed among the children of Israel.

III.

1. The fame of the riches of Israel spread over

all the world, and the neighboring nations envied them.

2. But the victorious arms of the Hebrews were directed by the Most High himself, and the pagans dared not attack them.

3. Unhappily as man does not always obey even his own will, the fidelity of the Israelites to their God was not of long duration.

4. They began by forgetting all the favors he had showered upon them, invoked his name on rare occasions only, and begged protection of magicians and wizards;

5. The kings and rulers substituted their own laws for those that Mossa had prepared; the temple of God and the practice of religion were abandoned, the nation gave itself up to pleasures and lost its original purity.

6. Many centuries had elapsed since their departure from Egypt, when God again resolved to punish them.

7. Strangers began to invade the land of Israel,

devastating the fields, destroying the villages, and taking the inhabitants into captivity.

8. A throng of pagans came from over the sea, from the country of Romeles; they subjected the Hebrews, and the commanders of the army governed them by authority of Cæsar.

9. The temples were destroyed, the people were forced to abandon their worship of the invisible God and to sacrifice victims to pagan idols.

10. Warriors were made of the nobles; the women were ravished from their husbands; the lower classes, reduced to slavery, were sent by thousands beyond the seas.

11. As to the children, all were put to the sword; soon, through all the land of Israel, nothing was heard but weeping and wailing.

12. In this dire distress the people remembered their powerful God; they implored his mercy and besought him to forgive them; our Father, in his inexhaustible goodness, heeded their prayers.

IV.

1. And now the time had come, which the Supreme Judge, in his boundless clemency, had chosen to incarnate himself in a human being.

2. And the Eternal Spirit, which dwelt in a state of complete inertness and supreme beatitude, awakened and detached itself from the Eternal Being for an indefinite period,

3. In order to indicate, in assuming the human form, the means of identifying ourselves with the Divinity and of attaining eternal felicity.

4. And to teach us, by his example, how we may reach a state of moral purity and separate the soul from its gross envelope, that it may attain the perfection necessary to enter the Kingdom of Heaven which is immutable and where eternal happiness reigns.

5. Soon after, a wonderful child was born in the land of Israel; God himself, through the mouth of this child, spoke of the nothingness of the body and of the grandeur of the soul.

6. The parents of this new-born child were poor people, belonging by birth to a family of exalted piety, which disregarded its former worldly greatness to magnify the name of the Creator and thank him for the misfortunes with which he was pleased to try them.

7. To reward them for their perseverance in the path of truth, God blessed the first-born of this family; he chose him as his elect, and sent him forth to raise those that had fallen into evil, and to heal them that suffered.

8. The divine child, to whom was given the name of Issa, commenced even in his most tender years to speak of the one and indivisible God, exhorting the people that had strayed from the path of righteousness to repent and purify themselves of the sins they had committed.

9. People came from all parts to listen and marvel at the words of wisdom that fell from his infant lips; all the Israelites united in proclaiming that the Eternal Spirit dwelt within this child.

10. When Issa had attained the age of thirteen, when an Israelite should take a wife,

11. The house in which his parents dwelt and earned their livelihood in modest labor, became a meeting place for the rich and noble, who desired to gain for a son-in-law the young Issa, already celebrated for his edifying discourses in the name of the Almighty.

12. It was then that Issa clandestinely left his father's house, went out of Jerusalem, and, in company with some merchants, traveled toward Sindh

13. That he might perfect himself in the divine word and study the laws of the great Buddhas.

V.

1. In the course of his fourteenth year, young Issa, blessed by God, journeyed beyond the Sindh and settled among the Aryas in the beloved country of God.

2. The fame of his name spread along the Northern Sindh. When he passed through the country of the five rivers and the Radjipoutan, the worshipers of the god Djaïne begged him to remain in their midst.

3. But he left the misguided admirers of Djaïne and visited Juggernaut, in the province of Orsis, where the remains of Viassa-Krichna rest, and where he received a joyous welcome from the white priests of Brahma.

4. They taught him to read and understand the Vedas, to heal by prayer, to teach and explain the Holy Scripture, to cast out evil spirits from the body of man and give him back human semblance.

5. He spent six years in Juggernaut, Rajegriha, Benares, and the other holy cities; all loved him, for Issa lived in peace with the Vaisyas and the Soudras, to whom he taught the Holy Scripture.

6. But the Brahmans and the Kshatriyas declared that the Great Para-Brahma forbade them to approach those whom he had created from his entrails and from his feet:

7. That the Vaisyas were authorized to listen only to the reading of the Vedas, and that never save on feast days.

THE LIFE OF SAINT ISSA. 109

8. That the Soudras were not only forbidden to attend the reading of the Vedas, but to gaze upon them even; for their condition was to perpetually serve and act as slaves to the Brahmans, the Kshatriyas, and even to the Vaisyas.

9. "Death alone can free them from servitude," said Para-Brahma. "Leave them, therefore, and worship with us the gods who will show their anger against you if you disobey them."

10. But Issa would not heed them; and going to the Soudras, preached against the Brahmans and the Kshatriyas.

11. He strongly denounced the men who robbed their fellow-beings of their rights as men, saying: "God the Father establishes no difference between his children, who are all equally dear to him."

12. Issa denied the divine origin of the Vedas and the Pouranas, declaring to his followers that one law had been given to men to guide them in their actions.

13. "Fear thy God, bow down the knee before

Him only, and to Him only must thy offerings be made."

14. Issa denied the Trimourti and the incarnation of Para-Brahma in Vishnou, Siva, and other gods, saying:

15. "The Eternal Judge, the Eternal Spirit, composes the one and indivisible soul of the universe, which alone creates, contains, and animates the whole."

16. "He alone has willed and created, he alone has existed from eternity and will exist without end; he has no equal neither in the heavens nor on this earth."

17. "The Great Creator shares his power with no one, still less with inanimate objects as you have been taught, for he alone possesses supreme power."

18. "He willed it, and the world appeared; by one divine thought, he united the waters and separated them from the dry portion of the globe. He is the cause of the mysterious life of

man, in whom he has breathed a part of his being."

19. "And he has subordinated to man, the land, the waters, the animals, and all that he has created, and which he maintains in immutable order by fixing the duration of each."

20. "The wrath of God shall soon be let loose on man, for he has forgotten his Creator and filled his temples with abominations, and he adores a host of creatures which God has subordinated to him."

21. "For, to be pleasing to stones and metals, he sacrifices human beings in whom dwells a part of the spirit of the Most High."

22. "For he humiliates them that labor by the sweat of their brow to gain the favor of an idler who is seated at a sumptuously spread table."

23. "They that deprive their brothers of divine happiness shall themselves be deprived of it, and the Brahmans and the Kshatriyas shall become the Soudras of the Soudras with whom the Eternal shall dwell eternally."

24. "For on the day of the Last Judgment, the Soudras and the Vaisyas shall be forgiven because of their ignorance, while God shall visit his wrath on them that have arrogated his rights."

25. The Vaisyas and the Soudras were struck with admiration, and demanded of Issa how they should pray to secure their happiness.

26. "Do not worship idols, for they do not hear you; do not listen to the Vedas, where the truth is perverted; do not believe yourself first in all things, and do not humiliate your neighbor."

27. "Help the poor, assist the weak, harm no one, do not covet what you have not and what you see in the possession of others."

VI.

1. The white priests and the warriors becoming cognizant of the discourse addressed by Issa to the Soudras, resolved upon his death and sent their servants for this purpose in search of the young prophet.

THE LIFE OF SAINT ISSA. 113

2. But Issa, warned of this danger by the Soudras, fled in the night from Juggernaut, gained the mountains, and took refuge in the Gothamide Country, the birth-place of the great Buddha Cakya-Mouni, among the people who adored the only and sublime Brahma.

3. Having perfectly learned the Pali tongue, the just Issa applied himself to the study of the sacred rolls of Soutras.

4. Six years later, Issa, whom the Buddha had chosen to spread his holy word, could perfectly explain the sacred rolls.

5. He then left Nepal and the Himalaya Mountains, descended into the valley of Rajipoutan and went westward, preaching to divers people of the supreme perfection of man,

6. And of the good we must do unto others, which is the surest means of quickly merging ourselves in the Eternal Spirit. "He who shall have recovered his primitive purity at death," said Issa, "shall have obtained the forgiveness of his sins, and shall have the right to contemplate the majestic figure of God."

7. In traversing the pagan territories, the divine Issa taught the people that the adoration of visible gods was contrary to the laws of nature.

8. "For man," said he, "has not been favored with the sight of the image of God nor the ability to construct a host of divinities resembling the Eternal."

9. "Furthermore, it is incompatible with the human conscience to think less of the grandeur of divine purity than of animals; or of works made by the hand of man from stone or metal."

10. "The Eternal Legislator is one; there is no God but him; he has shared the world with no one, neither has he confided his intentions to anyone."

11. "Just as a father may deal toward his children, so shall God judge men after death according to his merciful laws; never will he humiliate his child by causing his soul to emigrate, as in a purgatory, into the body of an animal."

12. "The heavenly law," said the Creator through the lips of Issa, "is averse to the sacri-

fice of human victims to a statue or animal; for I have sacrificed to man all the animals and everything the world contains."

13. "Everything has been sacrificed to man, who is directly and closely linked to Me, his Father; therefore, he that shall have robbed Me of My child shall be severely judged and punished according to the divine law."

14. "Man is as nothing before the Eternal Judge, to the same degree that the animal is before man."

15. "Therefore, I say to you, abandon your idols and perform no ceremonies that separate you from your Father and bind you to priests from whom the face of heaven is turned away."

16. "For it is they who have allured you from the true God, and whose superstitions and cruelty are leading you to perversion of the intellect and the loss of all moral sense."

VII.

1. The words of Issa spread among the pagans,

in the countries through which he traveled, and the inhabitants abandoned their idols.

2. Seeing which, the priests demanded from him who glorified the name of the true God, proofs of the accusations he brought against them and demonstration of the worthlessness of idols in the presence of the people.

3. And Issa replied to them: "If your idols and your animals are mighty, and really possess a supernatural power, let them annihilate me on the spot!"

4. "Perform a miracle," retorted the priests, "and let thy God confound our own, if they are loathsome to him."

5. But Issa then said: "The miracles of our God began when the universe was created; they occur each day, each instant; whosoever does not see them is deprived of one of the most beautiful gifts of life."

6. "And it is not against pieces of inanimate stone, metal, or wood, that the wrath of God shall find free vent, but it shall fall upon man,

THE LIFE OF SAINT ISSA. 117

who, in order to be saved, should destroy all the idols they have raised."

7. "Just as a stone and a grain of sand, worthless in themselves to man, await with resignation the moment when he shall take and make them into something useful."

8. "So should man await the great favor to be granted him by God in honoring him with a decision."

9. "But woe be to you, adversary of man, if it be not a favor that you await, but rather the wrath of Divinity; woe be to you if you await until it attests its power through miracles!"

10. "For it is not the idols that shall be annihilated in His wrath, but those that have raised them; their hearts shall be the prey of everlasting fire, and their lacerated bodies shall serve as food for wild beasts."

11. "God shall drive away the contaminated ones of his flocks, but shall take back to himself those that have strayed because they misconceived the heavenly atom which dwelt in them."

12. Seeing the powerlessness of their priests, the pagans believed the words of Issa, and fearing the wrath of the Divinity, broke their idols into fragments; as to the priests, they fled to escape the vengeance of the people.

13. And Issa also taught the pagans not to strive to see the Eternal Spirit with their own eyes, but to endeavor to feel it in their hearts, and, by a truly pure soul, to make themselves worthy of its favors.

14. "Not only must you desist from offering human sacrifices," said he, "but you must immolate no animal to which life has been given, for all things have been created for the benefit of man."

15. "Do not take what belongs to others, for it would be robbing your neighbor of the goods he has acquired by the sweat of his brow."

16. "Deceive no one, that you may not yourself be deceived; strive to justify yourself before the last judgment, for it will then be too late."

17. "Do not give yourself up to debauchery, for it is a violation of the laws of God."

THE LIFE OF SAINT ISSA. 119

18. "You shall attain supreme beatitude, not only by purifying yourself, but also by leading others into the path that shall permit them to regain primitive perfection."

VIII.

1. The fame of Issa's sermons spread to the neighboring countries, and, when he reached Persia, the priests were terrified and forbade the inhabitants to listen to him.

2. But when they saw that all the villages welcomed him with joy, and eagerly listened to his preaching, they caused his arrest and brought him before the high-priest, where he was submitted to the following interrogatory:

3. "Who is this new God of whom thou speaketh? Dost thou not know, unhappy man that thou art, that Saint Zoroaster is the only just one admitted to the honor of receiving communications from the Supreme Being,

4. "Who has commanded the angels to draw up in writing the word of God, laws that were given to Zoroaster in paradise?"

5. "Who then art thou that darest to blaspheme our God and sow doubt in the hearts of believers?"

6. And Issa replied: "It is not of a new god that I speak, but of our heavenly Father, who existed before the beginning and will still be after the eternal end."

7. "It was of him I spoke to the people, who, even as an innocent child, can not yet understand God by the mere strength of their intelligence and penetrate his spiritual and divine sublimity."

8. "But, as a new-born child recognizes the maternal breast even in obscurity, so your people, induced in error by your erroneous doctrines and religious ceremonies, have instinctively recognized their Father in the Father of whom I am the prophet."

9. "The Eternal Being says to your people through the intermediary of my mouth: 'You shall not adore the sun, for it is only a part of the world I have created for man.'"

10. "The sun rises that it may warm you dur-

THE LIFE OF SAINT ISSA. 121

ing your labor; it sets that it may give you the hours of rest I have myself fixed."

11. "It is to Me, and to Me only, that you owe all you possess, all that is around you, whether above or beneath you."

12. "But," interjected the priests, "how could a nation live according to the laws of justice, if it possessed no preceptors?"

13. Then Issa replied: "As long as the people had no priests, they were governed by the law of nature and retained their candor of soul."

14. "Their souls were in God, and to communicate with the Father, they had recourse to the intermediary of no idol or animal, nor to fire, as you practice here."

15. "You claim that we must worship the sun, the genius of Good and that of Evil; well, your doctrine is an abomination, I say to you, the sun acts not spontaneously, but by the will of the Invisible Creator who has given it existence,

16. "And who has willed that this orb should

light the day and warm the labor and the crops of man."

17. "The Eternal Spirit is the soul of all that is animated; you commit a grievous sin in dividing it into the spirit of Evil and the spirit of Good, for there is no God save that of good,

18. "Who, like the father of a family, does good only to his children, forgiving all their faults if they repent of them."

19. "And the spirit of Evil dwells on this earth, in the heart of men who turn the children of God from the right path."

20. "Therefore I say to you, beware of the day of judgment, for God will inflict a terrible punishment on all who have turned his children from the right path and filled them with superstitions and prejudices,"

21. "On them that have blinded the seeing, transmitted contagion to the sound of health, and taught the adoration of things which God has subjected to man for his own good and to aid him in his labor."

22. "Your doctrine is therefore the fruit of your errors, for, in desiring to approach the God of Truth, you have created false gods."

23. After listening to him, the wise men resolved to do him no harm. In the night, while the city was wrapped in slumber, they conducted him outside the walls and left him on the highway, hoping that he might soon become the prey of wild beasts.

24. But, being protected by the Lord our God, Saint Issa continued his way unmolested.

IX.

1. Issa, whom the Creator had chosen to recall the true God to the people that were plunged in depravities, was twenty-nine years of age when he arrived in the land of Israel.

2. Since the departure of Issa, the pagans had heaped still more atrocious sufferings on the Israelites, and the latter were a prey to the deepest gloom.

3. Many among them had already begun to desert the laws of their God and those of Mossa, in the hope of softening their harsh conquerors.

4. In the presence of this situation, Issa exhorted his compatriots not to despair, because the day of the redemption of sins was near, and he confirmed their belief in the God of their fathers.

5. "Children, do not yield to despair," said the Heavenly Father through the mouth of Issa, "for I have heard your voices, and your cries have ascended to me."

6. "Weep not, O my beloved, for your sobs have touched the heart of your Father, and he has forgiven you as he forgave your ancestors."

7. "Do not abandon your families to plunge into debauchery, do not lose the nobility of your sentiments and worship idols that will remain deaf to your voices."

8. "Fill my temple with your hopes and your patience, and do not abjure the religion of your fathers, for I alone have guided them and heaped blessings upon them."

THE LIFE OF SAINT ISSA. 125

9. "Raise them that have fallen, feed them that are hungry, and help them that are sick, that you may all be pure and just on the day of the last judgment that I am preparing for you."

10. The Israelites flocked to hear the words of Issa, asking him where they should thank the Heavenly Father, since their enemies had razed their temples and laid violent hands on their sacred vessels.

11. Issa replied to them that God did not speak of temples built by the hands of men, but that he meant thereby the human heart, which is the true temple of God.

12. "Enter into your temple, into your own heart, illuminate it with good thoughts, patience, and the unflinching confidence you should place in your Father."

13. "And your sacred vessels are your hands and your eyes; look and do what is agreeable to God, for, in doing good to your neighbor, you perform a rite that embellishes the temple in which dwells the One who has given you life."

14. "For God has created you in his image; innocent, pure of soul, with a heart filled with kindness, and destined, not to the conception of evil projects, but to be the sanctuary of love and justice."

15. "Do not therefore sully your hearts, I say to you, for the Eternal Being dwells there always."

16. "If you wish to accomplish works stamped with love and piety, do them with an open heart, and let not your actions be inspired by the hope of gain or by thought of profit."

17. "For such deeds would not contribute to your salvation, and you would then fall into a state of moral degradation in which theft, falsehood, and murder, seem like generous actions."

X.

1. Saint Issa went from place to place strengthening, by the word of God, the courage of the Israelites, who were ready to succumb under the weight of their despair, and thousands followed him to hear his preaching.

THE LIFE OF SAINT ISSA. 127

2. But the rulers of the cities feared him, and word was sent to the Governor, who resided in Jerusalem, that a man named Issa had come into the country, that his sermons excited the people against the authorities, that the crowd listened to him assiduously and neglected their duties to the State, claiming that soon they would be rid of their intruding rulers.

3. Then Pilate, the Governor of Jerusalem, ordered that the preacher Issa be arrested, brought to the city and conducted before the judges; not to arouse the dissatisfaction of the people, however, Pilate commanded the priests and the learned men, old men of Hebrew origin, to judge him in the temple.

4. Meanwhile, Issa, still continuing to preach, arrived in Jerusalem; having heard of his coming all the inhabitants, who already knew him by reputation, came to meet him.

5. They greeted him respectfully and threw open the doors of their temple that they might hear from his lips what he had said in the other cities of Israel.

6. And Issa said to them: "The human race is perishing because of its want of faith, for the gloom and the tempest have bewildered the human flock, and they have lost their shepherd."

7. "But tempests do not last forever, and the clouds will not hide the eternal light, the heavens shall soon be serene again, the celestial light shall spread throughout the world, and the strayed sheep shall gather around their shepherd."

8. "Do not strive to seek direct roads in the obscurity for fear of stumbling into the ditch, but gather your remaining strength, sustain one another, place your entire trust in God, and wait till a streak of light appears."

9. "He that upholds his neighbor upholds himself, and whosoever protects his family protects his race and his country."

10. "For rest assured that the day of your deliverance from darkness is near; you shall gather together in one single family, and your enemy — he who knows nothing of the favor of the Great God — will tremble in fear."

THE LIFE OF SAINT ISSA. 129

11. The priests and the old men that listened to him, full of admiration at this language, asked of him if it were true that he had attempted to arouse the people against the authorities of the country, as had been reported to the Governor, Pilate.

12. "Is it possible to arise against misled men from whom the obscurity has hidden their path and their door?" returned Issa. "I have only warned these unfortunate people, as I warn them in this temple, that they may not advance further on their dark paths, for an abyss is yawning beneath their feet."

13. "Worldly power is not of long duration, and it is subject to innumerable changes. It would be of no use to a man to rebel against it, for one power always succeeds another power, and it shall be thus until the extinction of human existence."

14. "Do you not see, on the contrary, that the rich and the powerful are sowing among the children of Israel a spirit of rebellion against the eternal power of heaven?"

15. And the learned men then said: "Who art thou, and from what country hast thou come into our own? We had never heard of thee, and do not even know thy name."

16. "I am an Israelite," responded Issa, "and, on the very day of my birth, I saw the walls of Jerusalem, and I heard the weeping of my brothers reduced to slavery, and the moans of my sisters carried away by pagans into captivity."

17. "And my soul was painfully grieved when I saw that my brothers had forgotten the true God; while yet a child, I left my father's house to go among other nations."

18. "But hearing that my brothers were enduring still greater tortures, I returned to the land in which my parents dwelt, that I might recall to my brothers the faith of their ancestors, which teaches us patience in this world that we may obtain perfect and sublime happiness on High."

19. And the learned old men asked him this question: "It is claimed that you deny the laws of Mossa and teach the people to desert the temple of God?"

20. And Issa said: "We can not demolish what has been given by our Heavenly Father and what has been destroyed by sinners; but I have recommended the purification of all stain from the heart, for that is the veritable temple of God."

21. "As to the laws of Mossa, I have striven to re-establish them in the heart of men; and I say to you, that you are in ignorance of their true meaning, for it is not vengeance, but forgiveness that they teach; but the sense of these laws have been perverted."

XI.

1. Having heard Issa, the priests and learned men decided among themselves that they would not judge him, for he was doing no one harm, and having presented themselves before Pilate, made Governor of Jerusalem by the pagan king of the land of Romeles, they spoke to him thus:

2. "We have seen the man whom thou accusest of inciting our people to rebellion, we have heard his preaching and know that he is of our people."

3. "But the rulers of the towns have sent thee false reports, for he is a just man who teaches the people the word of God. After interrogating him, we dismissed him that he might go in peace."

4. The Governor overcome with passion sent disguised servants to Issa, that they might watch all his actions and report to the authorities every word he addressed to the people.

5. Nevertheless Issa continued to visit the neighboring towns and preach the true ways of the Creator, exhorting the Hebrews to patience and promising them a speedy deliverance.

6. And during all this time, a multitude followed wherever he went, many never leaving him and acting as servants.

7. And Issa said to them: "Do not believe in miracles performed by the hands of man, for He who dominates nature is alone capable of doing supernatural things, while man is powerless to soften the violence of the wind and bestow rain."

8. "Nevertheless, there is a miracle which it is possible for man to accomplish; it is when, full of a sincere faith, he resolves to tear from his heart all evil thought and, to attain his end, shuns the paths of iniquity."

9. "And all things which are done without God are but gross errors, seductions, and illusions, which only demonstrate to what point the soul of the man who practices this art is filled with deceit, falsehood, and impurity."

10. "Put no faith in oracles, God alone knows the future; he that has recourse to sorcerers defiles the temple within his heart and gives proof of distrust toward his Creator."

11. "Faith in sorcerers and their oracles destroys the innate simplicity and child-like purity in man; a diabolical power takes possession of him and forces him to commit all sorts of crimes and to adore idols."

12. "While the Lord our God, who has not his equal, is one, all-powerful, omniscient, and omnipresent; it is he who possesses all wisdom and all light."

13. "It is to him you must have recourse to be comforted in your sorrows, assisted in your toils, healed in your sickness; whosoever shall have recourse to him shall not be refused."

14. "The secret of nature is in the hands of God; for the world before appearing, existed in the depth of the divine mind; it became material and visible by the will of the Most High."

15. "When you wish to address him, become as children once more, for you know neither the past, nor the present, nor the future, and God is the master of time."

XII.

1. "O just man," said the disguised servants of the Governor of Jerusalem, "tell us should we do the will of our Cæsar or await our near deliverance?"

2. And Issa, having recognized in his questioners the spies sent to watch him, said to them: "I have not said that you should be delivered from Cæsar; it is the soul plunged in error which shall have its deliverance."

THE LIFE OF SAINT ISSA. 135

3. "There can be no family without a head, and there would be no order in a nation without a Cæsar, who must be blindly obeyed, for he alone shall answer for his actions before the supreme tribunal."

4. "Does Cæsar possess a divine right," again questioned the spies, "and is he the best of mortals?"

5. "There is no perfection among men, but there are also some that are sick whom the men elected and intrusted with this mission must care for, by using the means that are conferred upon them by the sacred law of our Heavenly Father."

6. "Clemency and justice, these are the highest gifts granted to Cæsar; his name will be illustrious if he abides thereby."

7. "But he who acts otherwise, who goes beyond the limit of his power over his subject, even to placing his life in danger, offends the great Judge and lowers his dignity in the sight of men."

136 UNKNOWN LIFE OF CHRIST.

8. At this point, an aged woman, who had approached the group that she might better hear Issa, was pushed aside by one of the men in disguise who placed himself before her.

9. Issa then said: "It is not meet that a son should push aside his mother to occupy the first place which should be hers. Whosoever respecteth not his mother, the most sacred being next to God, is unworthy the name of son."

10. "Listen, therefore, to what I am about to say: "Respect woman, for she is the mother of the universe and all the truth of divine creation dwells within her."

11. "She is the basis of all that is good and beautiful, as she is also the germ of life and death. On her depends the entire existence of man, for she is his moral and natural support in all his works."

12. "She gives you birth amid sufferings; by the sweat of her brow she watches over your growth, and until her death you cause her the most intense anguish. Bless her and adore her, for she is your only friend and support upon earth."

THE LIFE OF SAINT ISSA. 137

13. "Respect her, protect her; in doing this, you will win her love and her heart, and you will be pleasing to God; for this shall many of your sins be remitted."

14. "Therefore, love your wives and respect them, for to-morrow they shall be mothers, and later grandmothers of a whole nation."

15. "Be submissive toward your wife; her love ennobles man, softens his hardened heart, tames the beast and makes of it a lamb."

16. "The wife and the mother, inestimable treasures bestowed on you by God; they are the most beautiful ornaments of the universe, and from them shall be born all that shall inhabit the world."

17. "Just as the God of armies separated day from night and the land from the waters, so woman possesses the divine talent of separating good intentions from evil thoughts in men."

18. Therefore I say to you: "After God, your best thoughts should belong to women and to wives; woman being to you the divine temple

wherein you shall most easily obtain perfect happiness."

19. "Draw your moral strength from this temple; there you will forget your sorrows and failures, you will recover the wasted forces necessary to help your neighbor."

20. "Do not expose her to humiliation; you would thereby humiliate yourself and lose the sentiment of love, without which nothing exists here below."

21. "Protect your wife, that she may protect you and all your family; all that you shall do for your mother, your wife, for a widow, or another woman in distress, you shall have done for God."

XIII.

1. Saint Issa thus taught the people of Israel for three years in every city, in every village, on the roadways, and in the fields, and all that he had predicted came to pass.

2. During all this time, the disguised servants of the Governor Pilate observed him closely, but

THE LIFE OF SAINT ISSA. 139

without hearing anything that resembled the reports hitherto sent by the rulers of the cities concerning Issa.

3. But the Governor Pilate, becoming alarmed at the too great popularity of Saint Issa, who, according to his enemies, wanted to incite the people and be made king, ordered one of his spies to accuse him.

4. Soldiers were then sent to arrest him, and he was cast into a dungeon where he was made to suffer various tortures that he might be forced to accuse himself, which would permit them to put him to death.

5. Thinking of the perfect beatitude of his brothers only, the saint endured these sufferings in the name of his Creator.

6. The servants of Pilate continued to torture him and reduced him to a state of extreme weakness; but God was with him and did not suffer him to die.

7. Hearing of the sufferings and tortures inflicted on their saint, the principal priests and

140   UNKNOWN LIFE OF CHRIST.

learned elders begged the Governor to liberate Issa on the occasion of an approaching great feast.

8. But the Governor met them with a decided refusal. They then begged him to bring Issa before the tribunal of the Ancients, that he might be condemned or acquitted before the feast, to which Pilate consented.

9. On the morrow the Governor called together the chief rulers, priests, elders, and law-givers, with the object of making them pass judgment on Issa.

10. The saint was brought from his prison, and he was seated before the Governor between two thieves that were to be tried with him, to show the people that he was not the only one to be condemned.

11. And Pilate, addressing Issa, said: "O, man! is it true that thou hast incited the people to rebel against the authorities that thou mayest become king of Israel?"

12. "None can become king by his own will," replied Issa, "and they that have said that I

THE LIFE OF SAINT ISSA.   141

incited the people have spoken falsely. I have never spoken but of the King of Heaven, whom I taught the people to adore."

13. "For the sons of Israel have lost their original purity, and if they have not recourse to the true God, they shall be sacrificed and their temple shall fall in ruins."

14. "Temporal power maintains order in a country; I therefore taught them not to forget it; I said to them: "'Live in conformity to your position and fortune, that you may not disturb public order;' and I exhorted them also to remember that disorder reigned in their hearts and minds."

15. "Therefore the King of Heaven has punished them and suppressed their national kings; nevertheless, I said to them, if you resign yourself to your fate, the kingdom of heaven shall be reserved for you as a reward."

16. At this moment, witnesses were introduced; one of them testified as follows: "Thou hast said to the people that temporal power was noth-

ing to that of the King that shall free the Israelites from the pagan yoke."

17. "Blessed be thou," said Issa, "for having spoken the truth; the King of Heaven is more powerful and great than terrestrial laws, and his kingdom surpasses all the kingdoms here below."

18. "And the time is not far when, in conformity with the divine will, the people of Israel will purify themselves of their sins; for it is said that a precursor shall come to announce the deliverance of the nation and unite it in one family."

19. And addressing himself to the judges, the Governor said: "Hear you this? The Israelite Issa admits the crime of which he is accused. Judge him according to your laws and sentence him to capital punishment."

20. "We can not condemn him," replied the priests and the ancients; "thou hast thyself heard that he made allusion to the King of Heaven, and that he has preached nothing to the people which constitutes insubordination against the law."

21. The Governor then summoned the witness who, at the instigation of his master, Pilate, had betrayed Issa; and when this man came he addressed Issa thus: "Didst thou not claim to be the king of Israel in saying that the Lord of heaven had sent thee to prepare his people?"

22. And Issa having blessed him, said: "Thou shalt be forgiven, for what thou sayest cometh not of thee!" Then turning to the Governor, he continued: "Why lower thy dignity and teach thy inferiors to live in falsehood, since, even without this, thou hast the power to condemn an innocent man?"

23. At these words, the Governor became violently enraged and ordered the death of Issa, while he discharged the two thieves.

24. The judges, having deliberated among themselves, said to Pilate: "We will not take upon our heads the great sin of condemning an innocent man and of acquitting two thieves, a thing contrary to our laws."

25. "Do therefore as thou pleases." Having thus spoken, the priests and wise men went out

and washed their hands in a sacred vessel, saying: "We are innocent of the death of a just man."

XIV.

1. By order of the Governor, the soldiers seized upon Issa and the two thieves whom they conducted to the place of torture, where they nailed them to the crosses they had erected.

2. All that day, the bodies of Issa and of the two thieves remained suspended, dripping with blood, under the guard of soldiers; the people stood around about them, while the parents of the crucified men wept and prayed.

3. At sunset, the agony of Issa came to an end. He lost consciousness, and the soul of this just man detached itself from his body to become part of the Divinity.

4. Thus ended the terrestrial existence of the reflection of the Eternal Spirit, under the form of a man who had saved hardened sinners and endured so much suffering.

THE LIFE OF SAINT ISSA. 145

5. Pilate, however, becoming alarmed at his own actions, gave up the body of the holy man to his relations, who buried him near the place of his execution; the multitude then came to pray over his tomb and filled the air with weeping and wailing.

6. Three days later the Governor sent his soldiers to take up the body of Issa and bury it elsewhere, fearing a general uprising of the people.

7. The following day the sepulcher was found open and empty by the multitude; and the rumor immediately spread that the Supreme Judge had sent his angels to take away the mortal remains of the saint in whom dwelt on earth a part of the Divine Spirit.

8. When this report came to the ears of Pilate he fell into a rage and forbade everyone, under penalty of perpetual slavery, to ever utter the name of Issa and to pray to the Lord for him.

9. But the people continued to weep and praise their master aloud; therefore many were placed in captivity, subjected to torture, and put to death.

10. And the disciples of Saint Issa left the land of Israel and went in all directions among the pagans, telling them that they must abandon their gross errors, think of the salvation of their souls, and of the perfect felicity in store for men in the enlightened and immaterial world where, in repose and in all his purity, dwells the great Creator in perfect majesty.

11. The pagans, their kings and soldiers, listened to these preachers, abandoned their absurd beliefs, deserted their priests and their idols to sing the praises of the all-wise Creator of the universe, the King of kings, whose heart is filled with infinite mercy.

EPITOME.

IN reading the life of Issa (Jesus Christ), we are at first struck by the similarity between some of its principal passages and the biblical narrative; while, on the other hand, we also find equally remarkable contradictions, which constitute the difference between the Buddhist version and that found in the Old and New Testaments.

To explain this singularity, we must take into account the periods in which the facts were recorded.

In childhood, we were taught to believe that the Pentateuch was written by Moses himself; but the careful investigations of co-temporary savants have conclusively demonstrated, that in the days of Moses, and even long after him, there existed no writings in those countries bathed by the Mediterranean, save the Egyptian hieroglyphics and the cuneiform inscriptions still found in the excavations of Babylon. But we know, to the contrary, that the alphabet and parchment were known and used in China and India long before Moses.

Of this we have ample proof.

The sacred books of the "religion of the wise men," teaches us that the alphabet was invented in China, in 2800 B. C., by Fou-si, who was the first Chinese emperor to embrace that religion. It was he who also arranged the ritual and outward ceremonies. Yaou, the fourth Chinese emperor who adopted the same faith, published moral and civil laws, and, in the year 2228 B. C., prepared a penal code.

On his accession to the throne, Soune, the fifth emperor, proclaimed the "religion of the wise men" as the religion of state; and in 2282, he enacted new penal laws. These laws, modified by the Emperor Woo-Wang, who was the founder of the Chow dynasty in 1122, are now known under the name of the "Changes."

Moreover, the doctrine of Buddha-Fo, whose real name was Cakya-Mouni, was written on parchment. Foism began to spread through China about the year 260 B. C.; in 206, an emperor of the Tsine dynasty, who desired to study Buddhism, sent to India for the Buddhist Silifan; while the Emperor Ming-Ti, of the Han dynasty, one year before Christ, procured the sacred books written by Cakya-Mouni, the founder of Buddhism, who lived about the year 1200 before Christ.

EPITOME. 149

The doctrine of Buddha Gaouthama, or Gautama, who lived six hundred years before Christ, was written on parchment in the Pali language. At this epoch, there already existed in India about eighty-four thousand Buddhist manuscripts, the compiling of which must have required a considerable number of years.

While the Chinese and Hindoos already possessed a rich collection of written literature, the less fortunate, or more ignorant nations, who had no alphabet, transmitted orally, from generation to generation, what came to pass. Owing to the unreliability of the human memory, and its relative incapacity, not to speak of oriental embellishments, historical facts soon degenerated into fabulous legends, which, later, were gathered by unknown compilers and given to the world under the title of the "Five Books of Moses." The legend also attributes a truly extraordinary divine power to this Hebrew legislator, and credits him with a series of miracles performed in the presence of Pharaoh; might it not be equally mistaken in declaring that he was an Israelite by birth?

The Hindoo chroniclers, on the contrary, thanks to the invention of the alphabet, were enabled to preserve, not fabulous legends, but a concise narrative of recent events accomplished in their midst, as well as of the reports received from the merchants who had just visited foreign lands.

It is necessary to remark here that during this period of antiquity, as in our own days, oriental public life was concentrated in the bazaars, where the events of the day and the news from foreign nations were propagated by caravans of merchants, who were usually followed by a number of dervises who readily told all they had seen and heard on their journey, in exchange for food. In fact, this was their sole means of subsistence.

The commerce of India with Egypt, and later with Europe, was carried on through Jerusalem, where, even as early as the reign of Solomon, Hindoo caravans brought precious metals and all that was necessary for the construction of the temple. From Europe, the merchandise came to Jerusalem by sea, and was unloaded in the harbor where Jaffa now stands.

The chronicles in question were written before, during, and after Christ; although no attention was paid to Jesus during his sojourn in India, where he came as a simple pilgrim to study the Brahman and Buddhist laws.

But later, when the events which had aroused Israel were related in India, these chroniclers — after having committed to writing all they had

EPITOME.

just heard concerning the prophet Issa, whom an oppressed nation had followed and who had been executed by the order of Pilate—remembered that this same Issa had recently lived among them and studied in their midst, and that he had then returned to his own country. A deep interest was immediately aroused concerning this man who had so rapidly grown in importance in their eyes, and they at once began an investigation into his birth, his past, and every detail of his existence.

The two manuscripts read to me by the lama of the Himis Convent, were compiled from divers copies written in the Thibetan tongue, translated from rolls belonging to the Lassa library and brought from India, Nepal, and Maghada two hundred years after Christ. These were placed in a convent standing on Mount Marbour, near Lassa, where the Dalai-Lama now resides.

These rolls were written in the Pali tongue, which certain lamas study carefully that they may translate the sacred writings from that language into the Thibetan dialect.

The chroniclers were Buddhists belonging to the sect of Buddha Gautama.

The information contained about Christ is oddly mixed, without relation or coherence with other events of that period.

Without preliminary details or explanation, the manuscript begins by announcing that, in the very year of the death of Christ, a few merchants just returned from Judea have brought back the information that a just man named Issa, an Israelite, after having been twice acquitted by his judges — as was the man of God — was finally put to death at the instigation of the Pagan Governor, Pilate, who feared that Jesus would take advantage of his popularity to re-establish the Kingdom of Israel and expel its conquerors from the land.

Then comes the somewhat incoherent tale of Jesus preaching among the Guebers and other pagans, evidently written in the year following the death of Christ, in whom there is a growing interest. In one of these the merchants relate what is known of the origin of Jesus and of his family, while another gives the story of the expulsion of his partisans and the bitter persecutions they endured.

It is not until the end of the second volume is reached, that we find the first categorical affirmation of the chronicler where he declares that Issa is blessed by God and the best of all men; that he is the chosen one of the great Brahma, the man in whom is incarnated the spirit detached from the Supreme Being at a period determined by fate.

EPITOME.

Having explained that Issa was the son of poor parents and of Israelite extraction, the chronicler makes a slight digression with the object of telling us who were the children of Israel.

These fragments of the life of Issa, I have disposed of in chronological order, endeavoring to give them a character of unity totally wanting in the original form.

I leave to savants, philosophers, and theologians, the task of searching the cause of contradictions that may be found between the "Unknown Life of Issa," which I make public, and the story told by the Evangelists. But I am inclined to believe that nobody will hesitate to acknowledge that this version, recorded within three or four years after the death of Christ from the testimonies of eye witnesses, is more likely to bear the stamp of truth than the narratives of the Evangelists, who wrote at divers epochs, and so long a time after these events took place, that we can not be astonished if the facts have been altered or distorted.

Before taking up the life of Jesus, I must say a few words concerning the history of Moses, who, according to the usually accepted legend, was an Israelite. This fact is flatly contradicted by Buddhists. We are first told that Moses was a prince of Egypt, son of Pharaoh, and that he was merely instructed by the learned Israelites. By carefully examining this important point, we are forced to admit that the Buddhist author may be right.

Although I have no intention to destroy the biblical legend on the origin of Moses, many will concur with me in the opinion that Moses was not a simple Israelite, for the very appreciable reason that his education was that of a prince of the land; and it is difficult to believe that a child brought by chance into the palace, could have been placed on a footing of equality with the son of the sovereign. The manner in which the Egyptians treated their slaves proves that they were not distinguished for mildness of character. A foundling would assuredly not have been tolerated among the children of Pharaoh, but would have been placed with the servants. Besides, and this is preponderating evidence, we must take into consideration the spirit of caste so strictly observed in ancient Egypt.

On the other hand, it is difficult to believe that Moses did not receive a complete education. How otherwise could we explain his great work of legislation, his broad views, and his high qualities as administrator?

But, if he were a prince, why did he join the Israelites? The explanation is simple enough. We know that among the ancients, as well as in our modern days, the succession to the throne was frequently a bone of contention among brothers. Why not admit the hypothesis that Mossa, or Moses, wished to found a distinct kingdom, since the existence of an elder brother debarred him from the Egyptian throne? This consideration probably led him to place himself at the head of the Israelites, whom he admired for their firmness in their belief, as well as for their bodily strength. The Israelites of Egypt, we know, did not at all resemble their descendants physically, the blocks of granite used in building the palaces and the pyramids still stand as evidence of this.

The miracles performed in the presence of Pharaoh may be explained in the same way.

Without possessing definite arguments to deny these miracles performed by Moses, in the name of God, we must admit — without much difficulty, I believe — that the Buddhist verses are more plausible than the biblical paraphrase. The pest, small-pox, or cholera, must, in fact, have wrought terrible ravages in the dense mass of the population at a time when ideas on hygiene were still rudimentary, and when, in consequence, the scourge must have rapidly assumed frightful proportions.

Moses, who was of quick intelligence, could readily work on the fears of Pharaoh in the presence of this imminent danger, by declaring that it was due to the intervention of the God of Israel in favor of his chosen people.

This was a most favorable opportunity to free the Israelites from their bondage and make them pass under his own power.

Conformably to the will of Pharaoh, still, according to the Buddhists, Moses led the Israelites beyond the walls of the city; but, instead of building a new city at a certain distance from the capital, as he had been commanded to do, he took them out of the Egyptian territory. The indignation of Pharaoh on seeing Moses' utter disregard of his orders can be easily imagined; and it is not therefore astonishing if he started in pursuit of the fugitives at the head of his soldiers. Taking into consideration the geographical situation of that region, it must be supposed that Moses traveled along the mountains and entered Arabia through the isthmus now cut by the Suez Canal. Pharaoh, on the contrary, led his troops in a more direct line in the direction of the Red Sea; then, to overtake the Israelites who had already gained the opposite shore, he boldly took advantage of the ebb of the sea into the gulf formed by the banks of the isthmus, and made his soldiers march through the shallow passage. But the distance across being much longer than he had anticipated, the flood-tide caught the

Egyptian army in the very middle of the sea and not one of them could escape death.

This fact, so simple in itself, was transformed into a religious legend in the succeeding centuries by the Israelites, who interpreted the incident as due to divine intervention in their favor and as a just punishment from the hands of God on their persecutors. We are led to believe, moreover, that Moses himself entertained this belief. But this is a thesis which I shall endeavor to develop in a future work.

The Buddhist chronicle then briefly describes the greatness and the downfall of the kingdom of Israel, as well as its conquest by strangers who reduced its inhabitants to a state of servitude.

The misfortunes that poured upon the Israelites and the afflictions that thereafter embittered their days, were, according to the chronicler, more than sufficient reasons for God to look with pity upon his people; and, wishing to come to their assistance, he resolved to descend upon earth under the guise of a prophet, that he might lead them back into the path of salvation.

The condition of things at that period therefore justified the belief that the coming of Jesus was signaled, imminent, and necessary.

This explains why the Buddhist traditions declare that the Eternal Spirit detached itself from the Eternal Being and was incarnated in the new-born child of a pious and noble family.

The Buddhists, no doubt, as well as the Evangelists, wish to indicate thereby that the child belonged to the royal house of David; but the text of the Gospel, according to which the "child was conceived by the Holy Ghost," may be interpreted in two ways, while, according to the doctrine of Buddha, which is more in conformity with the laws of nature, the Spirit incarnated itself in a child that was already born, whom God blessed and chose to accomplish his mission here below.

At this point there is a void in the traditions of the Evangelists, who, whether through ignorance or negligence, tell us nothing of his infancy, his youth, and his education. They begin the history of Jesus by his first sermon, that is when, at the age of thirty, he returned to his own country.

All that is said by the Evangelists in regard to the infancy of Jesus is totally void of precision: "And the child grew, and waxed strong in spirit, filled with wisdom; and the grace of God was upon him," says one of the sacred authors, St. Luke, and again: "And the child grew, and waxed strong in spirit, and was in the deserts till the day of his shewing unto Israel."

As the Evangelists compiled their works long

after the death of Jesus, it is presumed that they merely consigned to writing the narratives that had come to them of the principal events of the life of Jesus.

The Buddhists, however, who compiled their chronicles immediately after the Passion, and who had the advantage of gathering the most accurate information on all points that interested them, give us a complete and exhaustive description of the life of Jesus.

In those unhappy days, when the struggle for existence seems to have destroyed all notion of God, the people of Israel were bowed down under the double oppression of the ambitious Herod, and of the avaricious despotic Romans. Then, as now, the Hebrews placed all their hope in Providence, which, they believed, would send them the inspired man who was to deliver them from their physical and moral sufferings. Time passed on, however, and no one took the initiative in a revolt against the tyranny of the governing power.

During this period of anxiety and hope, the people of Israel completely forgot that there existed in their midst a poor Israelite, who was a direct descendant of their King David. This poor man married a young girl who gave birth to a miraculous child.

Faithful to their traditions of devotion and respect for the race of their kings, the Hebrews, on hearing of this, flocked to see the child and congratulate the happy father. It is evident that Herod did not long remain in ignorance of what had taken place; and he feared that when the child had grown to manhood, he might take advantage of his popularity to regain the throne of his ancestors. He, therefore, sought the child, whom the Israelites endeavored to shield from the anger of the king; the latter then ordered the abominable massacre of children, hoping that Jesus might perish in this vast human hecatomb. But the family of Joseph, having obtained information of the terrible execution contemplated by Herod, fled into Egypt.

Some time later the family returned to its native land. The child had grown during these journeys in which his life had been more than once exposed. Then as now, the Oriental Israelites commenced to instruct their children at the age of five or six years. Forced to remain in concealment, the parents never allowed their son to leave their roof, and the latter no doubt spent his time in studying the sacred writings, so that on his return to Judea, he was far in advance of the boys of his own age, which greatly astonished the learned men. He was then in his thirteenth year, the age at which, according to the Jewish law, a young man attains his majority and has the right to marry, as well as to fulfill his religious duties on an equal footing with adults.

There still exists an ancient religious custom among the Israelites which fixes the majority of a man at the age of thirteen, when the youth enters society and enjoys the full privileges of his elders. His marriage at this age is considered absolutely legal and indispensable, even, in warm countries. In Europe, however, this custom has fallen into desuetude and lost its importance, owing to local laws, as well as to the laws of nature, which do not hasten physical development to the same degree as in warmer countries.

His royal origin, his rare intelligence, and the extensive studies to which he had applied himself, caused him to be looked upon as an excellent suitor, and the most noble and rich sought him as a son-in-law. So the Israelites of our days seek the honor of marrying their daughters to the son of a rabbi or a learned man. But the studious youth, seemingly detached from all things corporal and devoured by a thirst for knowledge, stealthily left his father's house and fled to India with a departing caravan.

It is to be supposed that Jesus Christ chose India, first, because Egypt made part of the

Roman possessions at that period, and then because an active trade with India had spread marvelous reports in regard to the majestic character and inconceivable riches of art and science in that wonderful country, where the aspirations of civilized nations still tend in our own age.

Here the Evangelists again lose the thread of the terrestrial life of Jesus. St. Luke says: "He was in the desert till the day of his shewing unto Israel," which conclusively proves that no one knew where the young man had gone, to so suddenly reappear sixteen years later.

Once in India, the country of marvels, Jesus began by frequenting the temples of the Djainites.

There still exists in the peninsula of Hindoostan a sect which bears the name of Djainism; it forms a link, as it were, between Buddhism and Brahmanism, and preaches the destruction of all other beliefs, which they declare to be steeped in error. It dates back to the seventh century before Christ, and its name is derived from the word "djaine" (conquering), which it assumes as a symbol of its triumph over its rivals.

Amazed at the young man's wonderful intellect, the Djainites begged him to remain in their midst; but Jesus left them to settle at Juggernaut, one of the principal cities of the Brahmans, and enjoying great religious importance at the time of Christ, where he devoted himself to the study of treatises on religion, philosophy, etc. A cherished tradition claims that the ashes of the illustrious Brahman Krichna are preserved here in the hollow of a tree near a magnificent temple visited by thousands every year. Krichna is supposed to have lived 1580 before Christ, and it was he who gathered and arranged the Vedas, dividing the work into four books: Richt, Jagour, Saman, and Artafan. This celebrated Brahman, who in recognition of this work received the name of Viassa (he who has gathered and divided the Vedas), also compiled the Vedantha and eighteen Pouranas, composed of four hundred thousand strophes.

A library, rich in Sanscrit books and precious religious manuscripts, is also found at Juggernaut.

Jesus spent six years at this place, studying the language of the country and the Sanscrit tongue, which enabled him to dive deeply into all religious doctrines, philosophy, medicine, and mathematics. He found much to condemn in Brahman laws and customs, and entered into public debates with the Brahmans, who strove to convince him of the sacred character of their established customs. Among other things, Jesus particularly censured the injustice of humiliating the laborer, and of not only depriving him of the benefits to come, but also of contesting his right to hear religious readings. And Jesus began to preach to the Soudras, the lowest caste of slaves, saying that God is one, according to their own laws, that all that is, exists through him, that all are equal in his sight, and that the Brahmans had obscured the great principle of monotheism in perverting the words of Brahma himself and insisting to excess on the exterior ceremonies of the religion.

These are the terms, according to the Brahman doctrine, in which God speaks of himself to the angels: "I have been since all eternity and shall be eternally. I am the first cause of all that exists in the East and in the West, in the North and in the South, above and below, in heaven and in hell. I am older than all things. I am the Spirit and the creation of the universe and its creator. I am all-mighty, I am the God of gods, the King of kings; I am Para-Brahma, the great soul of the universe."

After the world had appeared by the mere wish of Para-Brahma, God created men, whom he divided into four classes, according to their color: white (Brahmans), red (Kshatriyas), yellow (Vaisyas), and black (Soudras). Brahma drew the first from his own mouth, and gave them as their portion the government of the world, the teaching of the laws to men, and the power to heal and judge them. The Brahman alone, therefore, occupy the position of priests, and the preachers, or commentators of the Vedas only, must adopt celibacy.

The second caste, the Kshatriyas, came from the hand of Brahma. These he made warriors, intrusting them with the mission of defending and protecting society. The kings, princely rulers, governors, and troops, belong to this caste, which enjoys relations of the greatest cordiality with the Brahmans, because one can not exist without the other; and the peace of the country depends on the alliance of the sword and the light, of the temple of Brahma, and the royal throne.

The Vaisyas, who compose the third caste, were drawn by Brahma from his own entrails. They are destined to the plowing of the fields and the breeding of animals, to the exercise of all kinds of trades and commerce, that they may support the Brahmans and Kshatriyas. They are authorized to enter the temple and listen to the reading of the Vedas on feast days only, being obliged to remain at their business affairs on all other occasions.

The lowest caste, the blacks or Soudras, came from the feet of Brahma to be the humble servants and slaves of the three first castes. They are forbidden to attend the reading of the Vedas; and to come in contact with them means contamination. They are wretched beings, robbed of all human rights, not daring to even gaze at the members of the superior castes, or defend themselves, and, in case of sickness, deprived of the care of a physician.

Death alone can free them from the consequences of their life of servitude; but to obtain this reward they must, during their entire life, cheerfully and faithfully serve a member of one of the privileged classes. Then only, after having performed these functions with excessive zeal and fidelity in the service of a Brahman or a Kshatriya, can the Soudra entertain the hope that, after death, his soul shall be elevated to a superior caste.

Should a Soudra be found wanting in respect toward a member of the privileged classes, or otherwise merit disgrace, he is expelled from his caste, degraded to the rank of a pariah, and banished from cities and villages; he becomes an object of universal contempt, considered as an abject creature, and permitted to perform only the basest and most menial labor.

The same punishment may, it is true, be inflicted upon a member of any other caste; but by dint of repentance, of fastings and privations, the latter may in time regain their former rank, while the wretched Soudra is forever lost if once expelled from his caste.

It is therefore easy to understand the veneration of the Vaisyas and the Soudras for Jesus, who, notwithstanding the threats of the Brahmans, never abandoned them.

In his sermons, Jesus not only inveighed against the injustice of depriving a man of his right to be considered as such, while a monkey, or a piece of marble and metal was worshiped, but also denounced the main principle of Brahmanism, its system of gods, its doctrine, and its trimourti (trinity), the keystone of this religion.

Para-Brahma is represented with three faces on one single head: This is the trimourti (trinity), composed of Brahma (the creator), Vischnou (the preserver), and Siva (the destroyer).

The origin of the trimourti is as follows:

In the beginning, Para-Brahma created the waters and cast upon them the generating seed, which was transformed into a dazzling egg reflecting the image of Brahma. Millions of centuries later, Brahma divided this egg into two parts, the upper half of which became heaven and the lower half the earth. This done, Brahma came down upon this earth in the appearance of a child, placed himself on a lotus flower, withdrew within himself and propounded this question: "Who shall watch over the preservation of what I have created?" The answer came from his own mouth as flame: "I," and Brahma gave this word the name of Vischnou, which signifies, "he who preserves." Brahma then divided his being into two halves, one male and the other female, the active world and the passive world, the union of which brought forth Siva, "the destroyer."

The attributes of the trimourti are: Brahma, the creator being; Vischnou, the preserving wisdom; Siva, the destructive wrath of justice. Brahma is the substance from which all things are made; Vischnou, the space in which everything lives; and Siva, time which destroys all things.

Brahma is the face that animates everything; Vischnou, the water that sustains the strength of creatures; Siva, the fire that breaks the links that unite objects. Brahma is the past, Vischnou the present, and Siva the future. Each part of the trimourti, moreover, possesses a wife: That of Brahma is Sarasvati, goddess of wisdom; that of Vischnou is called Lackmi, goddess of virtue;

and Siva is married to Kali, goddess of death, the universal destroyer.

From this last union was born the wise god, Ganega, and Indra, chief of the inferior divinities, the number of which, including all objects of adoration belonging to the Hindoos, comes to three hundred millions.

Vischnou came down upon earth eight times, incarnating himself first in a fish, to save the sacred books from the deluge, then successively in a turtle, a dwarf, a wild boar, a lion, later in Rama — who was a king's son — in Krichna, and finally in Buddha. He will come a ninth time under the form of a cavalier mounted on a white horse, to destroy death and sin.

Jesus denied the existence of all these hierarchal absurdities of gods which obscured the great principle of monotheism.

Seeing that the people were beginning to embrace the doctrines of Jesus, whom they had hoped to gain on their side, and who was now their adversary, the Brahmans resolved to assassinate him; but being warned in time by his devoted servants, he fled and took refuge in the mountains of Nepal.

Buddhism had already taken deep root in this country at that period. This schism was remarkable for its moral principles and ideas on the nature of the divinity, which brought man and nature, and men among themselves, nearer together.

The founder of the sect, Cakya-Mouni, was born fifteen hundred years before Christ at Kapila, the capital of his father's kingdom, near Nepal in the Himalayas. He belonged to the Gothamide race and to the ancient family of Cakyas. He evinced a strong attachment to religion from childhood, and, notwithstanding his father's objections and disapproval, left the palace in which he lived with all its luxuries. He immediately began to preach against the Brahmans, meanwhile purifying their doctrine. He died at Koucinagara, surrounded by many of his faithful disciples. His body was burned, and his ashes distributed among the cities in which his new doctrine had replaced Brahmanism.

According to the Buddhist doctrine, the Creator always remains in a state of absolute inaction which nothing can disturb, and from which he arouses only at certain epochs determined by fate, in order to create terrestrial Buddhas. To this end, the Spirit is detached from the sovereign Creator and incarnated in a Buddha, in whom it dwells for some time on earth, where it creates buddhissatwas (masters) whose mission it is to preach the divine word and found new churches of believers, to whom they shall give laws and for whom they will institute a new religious order according to the traditions of Buddhism.

A terrestrial Buddha is, in some sort, a reflection of the sovereign Creator Buddha, to whom he again unites himself after the termination of his existence on earth; so it is with the Buddhissatwas who, as a reward for their works and the privations they have endured here below, receive eternal beatitude and enjoy a repose nothing can disturb.

Jesus spent six years among the Buddhists, where he found the principle of monotheism still in its purity. Having attained the age of twenty-six years he bethought himself of his native country, which labored under a foreign yoke. He therefore resolved to return there. While journeying thither he continued to preach against idolatry, human sacrifices, and religious errors, exhorting the people to acknowledge and adore God, the father of all creatures whom he cherishes equally, the masters as well as the slaves, for they are all his children, to whom he has given his beautiful universe as a common inheritance. The sermons of Jesus often produced a deep impression upon the nations he visited, where he braved many dangers instigated by the priests, but was as often protected by the idolaters, who, only the day before, had sacrificed their children to the idols.

While crossing Persia, Jesus almost caused an uprising among the followers of the doctrine of Zoroaster. Fearing the vengeance of the people, however, the priests dared not assassinate him, but had recourse to a ruse instead, and drove him from the town during the night, hoping he might be devoured by wild beasts. But Jesus escaped this peril and arrived safe and sound in the land of Israel.

It must be here remarked that the Orientals, in the midst of their picturesque wretchedness and the ocean of depravity in which they have sunk, under the continued influence of their priests and preceptors, possess nevertheless a most pronounced predilection for instruction and readily understand properly applied explanations. More than once, by the aid of some simple words of truth, I have successfully appealed to the conscience of a thief or an unruly servant. These people, moved by a sentiment of innate honesty, which the clergy, to further their own personal ends, endeavor by all possible means to stifle — these people, I repeat, are very quick to learn the principles of honesty, and exhibit the greatest contempt for those who have abused them.

By virtue of a single word of truth, it is possible to make of all India, with its three hundred millions of idols, a vast Christian country; but — this beautiful project would undoubtedly be prejudicial to certain Christians, who, like the aforesaid priests, speculate on the ignorance of the masses to enrich themselves.

Saint Luke says that: " Jesus was about thirty years of age when he began to exercise his ministry." According to the Buddhist chronicler, Jesus would have commenced to preach in his twenty-ninth year. All his sermons, which the Evangelists do not mention and which have been preserved by the Buddhists, are remarkable for their character of divine grandeur. The fame of the new preacher spread rapidly through the country, and Jerusalem impatiently awaited his coming. When he drew near to the holy city, all the inhabitants went forth to meet him and conducted him in triumph to the temple, which is in conformity with the Christian tradition. The chiefs and the learned men who listened, admired his sermons and rejoiced at the beneficent impression produced on the multitude by the words of Jesus. All the remarkable sermons of Jesus are filled with sublime words.

But Pilate, Governor of the country, did not see the matter in the same light. Zealous agents reported to him that Jesus announced the near approach of a new kingdom, the re-establishment of the throne of Israel, and that he called himself the Son of God, sent to revive the courage of Israel, for he, King of Judea, would soon ascend the throne of his ancestors.

I have no wish to attribute to Jesus the role of revolutionist, but, to me, it seems very probable that he labored with the people with a view of re-establishing the throne that was his by right of inheritance. Divinely inspired, and at the same time fully convinced that his pretensions were legitimate, Jesus therefore preached the spiritual union of the people that a political union might result.

Alarmed at these rumors, Pilate assembled the learned men and the elders of the people, charging them to interdict Jesus from public preaching and condemn him in the temple under the accusation of apostacy. This was the easiest way of ridding himself of a dangerous man whose royal origin was known to Pilate, and whose fame was growing among the people.

It must be remarked on this subject, that far from persecuting Jesus, the Israelites, recognizing in him the descendant of the illustrious dynasty of David, made him the object of their secret hopes, as is proved by the scripture, which relates that Jesus preached openly in the temple in the presence of the elders, who had the power to prohibit him, not only access to the temple, but even of preaching in public.

At Pilate's order, the Sanhedrim assembled and cited Jesus to appear before its tribunal. At the conclusion of the inquest, the members of the Sanhedrim announced to Pilate that his suspicions were groundless, that Jesus was propagating religious truths, and not political ideas; that he preached the divine word, and that, furthermore, he claimed to have come, not to overthrow, but to re-establish the laws of Moses. The Buddhist chronicle only tends to confirm this sympathy which indubitably existed between Jesus, the young preacher, and the elders of the people of Israel; hence their response: "We do not judge a just man."

Pilate was not reassured, however, and sought another opportunity of summoning Jesus before a regular tribunal; to this end, he sent many spies to watch him, and he was at length apprehended.

According to the Evangelists, it was the Pharisees and the Hebrews who sought to put Jesus to death, while the Buddhist chronicler positively declares that Pilate alone must be held responsible. This version is evidently much more likely than the account given by the Evangelists;

the conquerors of Judea being unable to long tolerate the presence of a man who announced to the people their near deliverance from the foreign yoke. The popularity of Jesus having proved disquieting to Pilate, it was but natural that he should dispatch spies with instructions to watch every word and action of the young preacher. In their character of inciting agents, these spies endeavored, by propounding embarrassing questions to Jesus, to force him to utter some imprudent words that might permit Pilate to proceed against him. Had Jesus' preaching displeased the wise men and Hebrew priests, they would simply have ordered the people not to listen to him or follow him, and have interdicted him entering the temple. The Evangelists, however, relate that Jesus enjoyed great freedom among the Israelites and in the temple, where Pharisees and learned men conversed with him.

That he might succeed in condemning him, Pilate submitted him to inquisition, hoping to drive him to an avowal of high treason.

Seeing that tortures did not bring about the desired result, and that, unlike other innocent persons put to the same suffering and agony, Jesus did not falter and accuse himself, Pilate commanded his servants to proceed to the utmost cruelty, that his death might be brought about by exhaustion. Jesus, however, finding a source of strength and courage in his own will and in his confidence in his cause, which was that of the nation and of God himself, opposed an unflinching endurance to all the refinements of cruelty received at the hands of his torturers.

Jesus having undergone the secret inquisition, the elders were much displeased thereat; they therefore resolved to intercede in his favor and ask that he be set at liberty before the feast of the Passover.

Foiled in the object of their demand by Pilate, they determined to insist upon having him brought before the tribunal, so certain were they of his acquittal, which seemed fully assured since the entire people ardently desired it.

In the eyes of the priests, Jesus was a saint belonging to the house of David, and his unjust detention, or what was still more grave, his condemnation, would cast a deep gloom upon the solemnity of the great national feast of the Israelites.

On learning of the refusal of their demand, they begged that the trial should take place before the feast. This time Pilate acceded to their wishes, but also ordered that two thieves should be tried at the same time. By this means Pilate strove to belittle, in the eyes of the people, the importance that might be attached to a judgment rendered against an innocent man if he were tried alone, thus leaving the nation under the sad impression of a verdict dictated beforehand; while, on the contrary, the simultaneous condemnation of Jesus and the two thieves would almost efface the injustice committed against one of the accused.

The accusation was based upon the depositions of hired witnesses.

During the trial, Pilate used the words of Jesus, who preached the Kingdom of Heaven, to justify the accusation against him. He counted, it would seem, upon the effect produced by the replies of Jesus, as well as on his own personal authority to influence the members of the tribunal to not examine too minutely the details of the case before them to obtain the desired verdict.

After hearing the perfectly natural reply of the judges, that the words of Jesus only proved a sentiment diametrically opposed to the accusation, and that he could not be condemned thereon, Pilate had recourse to the only means left him, that is, to the deposition of an informer, who, in the Governor's judgment, could not fail to produce a deep impression on the judges. The wretch, who was none other than Judas, then formally accused Jesus of having incited the people to rebellion.

Then followed a scene of the grandest sublimity. While Judas gave utterance to his testimony, Jesus turned to him, and, having blessed him, said: "Thou shalt be forgiven, for what thou sayest cometh not of thee." Then turning to the Governor, he continued: "Why lower thy dignity and teach thy inferiors to live in falsehood, since, even without this, thou hast the power to condemn an innocent man?"

Touching and sublime words! Jesus Christ manifests himself in all his grandeur, first in showing the informer that he has sold his conscience, then in forgiving him; turning next to Pilate, he censured him for having recourse to proceedings so degrading to his dignity to obtain his condemnation.

The accusation brought by Jesus against Pilate, caused the latter to completely forget his position and the prudence he should display; he therefore imperiously demanded the condemnation of Jesus at the hands of the judges, and, as if to assert the unlimited power he enjoyed, the acquittal of the two thieves.

Finding this demand to discharge the two thieves and condemn Jesus, though innocent, too unjust to comply with, the judges refused to commit this double crime against their conscience and their laws; but being too weak to struggle against a man who had the power to give a final verdict, and seeing him determined to rid himself of a person who rivaled the Roman authorities, they left him to pronounce the judgment he so ardently desired. That they might not be censured by the people, who could not have forgiven so unjust a judgment, they washed their hands as they came out of the tribunal chamber, showing thereby that they were innocent of the death of Jesus, whom the multitude adored.

About ten years ago I read an article on Judas in a German journal, the *Fremdenblatt*, in which the author endeavored to show that the informer had been Jesus' best friend. It would seem that it was through love for his master that Judas betrayed him, in his blind belief in the words of the Savior, who said that his kingdom would come after his crucifixion. But when he beheld him on the cross, after vainly awaiting his immediate resurrection, Judas found himself incapable of bearing his remorse and hanged himself.

It is useless to elaborate on this lucubration, which is certainly original.

But to return to the scriptural narrative and the Buddhist chronicle, it seems quite probable that the hired informer may have been Judas, although the Buddhist version is silent on this point. As to the theory that remorse of conscience drove the informer to the taking of his own life, I place little credence in it. A man capable of committing an act of such cowardice and of bringing against any one of his fellow-men an accusation so notoriously false, and that, not from a spirit of envy or revenge, but for a mere handful of silver, such a man, I repeat, is psychologically worthless. He is ignorant of all idea of honesty or conscience, and remorse is unknown to him.

It is to be presumed that the Governor took this matter into his own hands, as is sometimes done in our days, when it is imperative to keep from the people a grave and compromising secret which such a man might easily betray without heeding the consequences. Judas was no doubt hanged forthwith to prevent him from ever revealing that the testimony on which Jesus was condemned emanated from the Governor himself.

On the day of the crucifixion, a large body of Roman soldiers was stationed about the cross to prevent the people from rescuing the object of their worship. In this circumstance, Pilate displayed extraordinary firmness and resolution. But though, owing to his precautions, an uprising was averted, he could not prevent the people from weeping over the downfall of their hopes, which died with the last descendant of the house of David. The entire population went to adore the tomb of Jesus, and though we have no precise details of the first days after the Passion, we may easily imagine the scenes that must have taken place. It is only reasonable to suppose that the prudent lieutenant of the Roman Cæsar, seeing that the tomb of Jesus was becoming a shrine of universal lamentations and the object of national mourning, and fearing that the memory of this just man might excite discontent and perhaps arouse the entire population against their foreign yoke, should have taken all possible means to divert the public mind from the recollection of Jesus. For three days, the soldiers placed on guard at the tomb were the butt of the jeers and maledictions of the people, who, braving the danger, came in throngs to adore the great martyr. Pilate therefore ordered his soldiers to remove the body during the night, when the pilgrimages had ceased, and inter it clandestinely in another place, leaving the first tomb open and unguarded, that the people might see that Jesus had disappeared.

But Pilate failed to accomplish this end; for, on the following day, not finding the body of their master in the sepulcher, the Hebrews, who were very superstitious and believed in miracles, declared him resuscitated.

How this legend came to be generally accepted, we know not. It may have existed for a long time in a latent state and been first spread among the lower classes; or, perhaps, the Hebrew ecclesiastics looked with indulgence upon this innocent belief which gave to the oppressed a shadow of revenge against their oppressors. However this may be, since the day this legend of the resurrection became known to all, no one has had the strength of mind to point out the impossibility of it.

As concerns the resurrection itself, it must be remarked that, according to the Buddhists, the soul of the just man was united to the Eternal Being, while the Evangelists strongly insist upon the ascension of the body. It nevertheless seems to me, that the Evangelists and Apostles were wise in giving a plastic description of the resurrection; for otherwise, that is to say, had the miracle been less material, their sermons would not have been stamped, in the eyes of the people, with that divine authority, that character so manifestly divine which christianity retains to this day, as being the only religion capable of maintaining the people in a state of sublime enthusiasm, of softening their savage instincts, and of bringing them nearer to the great and simple nature which God has confided, it is said, to the feeble dwarf called man.

EXPLANATORY NOTES.

CHAPTER III.

§§ 3, 4, 5, 7.

THE history of all people shows that when a nation has attained the zenith of its riches and military glory, it almost immediately begins to slide more or less rapidly down the hill of decay and of moral decline. The Israelites were the first to undergo this law of the evolution of nations; and the neighboring countries took advantage of this to attack the effeminated and corrupted descendants of Jacob.

§ 8.

The country of Romeles — that is, the land of Romulus, or Rome, as it is called in our days.

§§ 11, 12.

It is evident that the Israelites, notwithstanding their incontestable genius and intelligence, never seemed to think of the morrow. Like all other oriental nations, it was only in their days of misfortune that they remembered their past sins, which they were each time obliged to redeem by centuries of slavery.

CHAPTER IV.

§ 6.

This verse, it is readily seen, refers to Joseph, who was a direct descendant of King David. This somewhat vague assertion bears some analogy to the following scriptural verses:

"Behold, the angel of the Lord appeared unto him in a dream, saying, Joseph, thou son of David, fear not to take unto thee Mary thy wife."—(Gospel according to St. Matthew i, 20.)

"And the multitudes that went before, and that followed, cried, saying, Hosanna to the son of David!"—(Gospel according to St. Matthew xxi, 9.)

"To a virgin espoused to a man whose name was Joseph, of the house of David."—(Gospel according to St. Luke i, 27.)

"And the Lord God shall give unto him the throne of his father David."—(Gospel according to St. Luke i, 32.)

"And Jesus himself began to be about thirty years of age, being (as was supposed) the son of Joseph, which was the son of Heli, which was the son of Nathan, which was the son of David."—(Gospel according to St. Luke iii, 23, 24, 25, 26, 27, 28, 29, 30, 31, etc.)

§ 7.

The Old and New Testaments teach us that God promised David that he would regenerate his throne and place one of his descendants upon it.

§§ 8, 9.

"And the child grew, and waxed strong in spirit, filled with wisdom; and the grace of God was upon him."

"And it came to pass, that after three days, they found him in the temple, sitting in the midst of the doctors, both hearing them, and asking them questions."

"And all that heard him were astonished at his understanding and answers."

"And he said unto them, How is it that ye sought me? wist ye not that I must be about my Father's business?"

"And Jesus increased in wisdom and stature, and in favour with God and man." (Gospel according to St. Luke ii, 40, 46, 47, 49, 52.)

CHAPTER V.

§ 1.

"Sind," a Sanscrit word, modified by the Persians into Ind; "Arya," ancient name of the inhabitants of India; it first signified "man who ploughs the soil," or

EXPLANATORY NOTES. 187

"husbandman;" in remote antiquity it possessed a purely ethnographic signification; but later, this appellation acquired a religious meaning, principally that of "man who believes."

§ 2.

St. Luke says (i, 80): "And the child grew, and waxed strong in spirit, and was in the desert till the day of his shewing unto Israel." The Evangelists say that Jesus remained in the desert; the Buddhists only explain the version of the scripture in indicating where Jesus lived during his absence from Judea; according to them, he crossed the Sind, a word which, properly speaking means "the stream" (the Indus). It is proper here to remark that many Sanscrit words have, in passing into the Persian tongue, undergone the same transformation of "s" into "h"; as for example:

Sapta (in Sanscrit), which signifies seven — hafta (in Persian).

Sam (in Sanscrit), which signifies equal — ham (in Persian).

Mas (in Sanscrit), which signifies mouth — mah (in Persian).

Sur (in Sanscrit), which signifies sun — hur (in Persian).

Das (in Sanscrit), which signifies ten — dah (in Persian).

Loco citato — and they that believed in the god Djaine.

There exists, even in our days, in the Peninsula of Hindoostan, a sect bearing the name of Djainism; it forms, as it were, a link between Buddhism and Brahmanism, and preaches the destruction of all other beliefs which, it is claimed, are impregnated with errors. It dates back to the seventh century before Christ; its name is derived from the word "Djaine" (conqueror), which it assumes as a symbol of triumph over its rivals.

§ 4.

Each of the eighteen Pouranas is divided into five parts, which, besides canonical laws, rites, and commentaries on the creation, the destruction, and resuscitation of the world, also treat of theogony, medicine, and of trades even.

CHAPTER VI.

§ 12.

It was only through the intervention of the English that an end was finally put to human sacrifices, offered principally to Kali, the goddess of death. The goddess Kali is represented standing, with one foot placed on the corpse of a man whose head she holds in one of her innumerable hands, while in another she grasps a bleeding sword. The wide-open mouth and eyes express passion and cruelty.

CHAPTER VIII.

§§ 3, 4.

Zoroaster lived five hundred and fifty years before Jesus Christ. He was founder of the doctrine of the struggle of light against darkness, a doctrine fully expounded in the Zend-Avesta (Word of God), written in the Zend tongue, and which, according to the legend, was given him by an angel in Paradise.

According to Zoroaster, we should worship Mithra (the sun), from which are descended the god of good, Ormuzd, and the god of evil, Ariman. The world is to come to an end when Ormuzd has triumphed over his rival, Ariman, who shall then return to his original source — Mithra.

CHAPTER X.

§ 16.

According to the Evangelists, Jesus was born in Bethlehem, which confirms the Buddhist version; for it is from Bethlehem only, seven kilometers from Jerusalem, that the walls of the latter city can be seen.

CHAPTER XI.

§ 15.

The doctrine of the Redemptor is nearly all contained

in the Gospels. As to the transformation of men into children, this is explained in the conversation between Jesus and Nicodemus.

CHAPTER XII.

§ 1.

"Tell us, therefore, What thinkest thou? Is it lawful to give tribute unto Cæsar, or not?" (Gospel according to St. Matthew xxii, 17).

§ 3.

Then Jesus replied: "Render therefore unto Cæsar the things which are Cæsar's, and unto God the things that are God's."

CHAPTER XIV.

§ 3.

According to the Buddhist belief, the terrestrial Buddhas at their death lose consciousness of their independent existence and become united to the Eternal Spirit.

§§ 10, 11.

Reference is, no doubt, here made to the apostles and their activity among the neighboring nations; an activity which, at that period, could not pass unperceived, because of the great results obtained by the preaching of new religious principles based on brotherly love, in the midst of people who professed religions founded on the cruelty of their gods.

Without permitting myself to indulge in long dissertations, or too deep analysis of each verse, I thought it only right to accompany my work with a few brief explanatory notes, leaving the reader to do as much for the remainder.

[END.]